# HOMES
## ON THE MOVE

MOBILE ARCHITECTURE     MOBILE ARCHITEKTUR

© h.f.ullmann publishing GmbH

*Editorial Project*: LiberLab, Italy (www.liberlab.it)
*Texts*: Donato Nappo, Stefania Vairelli (www.donatonappo.com)
*Layout*: Micaela Ballario, gi.mac grafica, Italy
*Typesetting*: Chiara Borda, LiberLab, Italy
*Coverdesign:* Simone Sticker on the basis of a layout by Micaela Ballario, gi.mac grafica, Italy

*Project coordination for h.f.ullmann*: Lars Pietzschmann

*Translation into English*:
Jim Potter for bookwise GmbH, Munich
*Translation into German*:
Daniela Papenberg for bookwise GmbH, Munich

*Overall responsibility for production*:
h.f.ullmann publishing GmbH, Potsdam, Germany

Printed in China, 2013

ISBN 978-3-8480-0477-5

10 9 8 7 6 5 4 3 2 1
X IX VIII VII VI V IV III II I

www.ullmann-publishing.com
newsletter@ullmann-publishing.com

# HOMES ON THE MOVE

## MOBILE ARCHITECTURE     MOBILE ARCHITEKTUR

**DONATO NAPPO & STEFANIA VAIRELLI**

h.f.ullmann

# index

# index

# index

# index

## Mobile architecture that adapts to any situation

*Homes on the Move* traces the global history of the temporary dwelling, from its earliest recorded origins to today's most modern solutions. We will show you that words like "house" or "fixed abode" are mere concepts that do not necessarily require walls, borders and roads to exist.

In ancient times, the ability to move at the drop of a hat was sometimes a necessity. For some that still holds true, but that necessity has became more of a choice in today's world. The concept of mobility, however, was never lost on architects, engineers and designers who enjoy the challenge of developing new housing solutions and construction techniques.

The first example of the mobile home was of course the tent. It was a nomad's shelter of choice across the deserts of Asia, the Americas and Africa. Utilized since antiquity, tents were given different names and shapes depending on the region. Among the most recognisable versions are the yurt, the tipi and the black tent.

# General Introduction – Allgemeine Einführung

The traditional house, as it is understood in the modern world, is formed of external walls, interior partitions and doors. The concept of prefabrication explored in this book is intended to liberate this model from the rigid and the static in order to make it transportable. It is a philosophy based on modular panels and factory-built units that can be assembled quickly on site.

## Mobile Architektur, die sich den momentanen Gegebenheiten anpasst

Homes on the Move *gibt einen Überblick über die Geschichte des flexiblen, mobilen Wohnens von den Anfängen bis heute in den unterschiedlichsten geografischen Gebieten. Dabei wird deutlich, dass „Wohnraum" als physischer Ort auf festgesetzte Mauern, auf Begrenzungen, eine Straße oder eine Siedlung verzichten kann.*

*Mit der eigenen Behausung jederzeit umziehen zu können stellte früher – und für einige Bevölkerungsgruppen noch heute – eine absolute Notwendigkeit dar. Durch das Aufkommen des Mobilitätskonzepts als freie Entscheidung und Lebensideal wird daraus zunehmend ein ambitioniertes Betätigungsfeld für Architekten, Ingenieure und Designer, das zum Experimentieren mit neuen Möglichkeiten und Bautechniken einlädt.*

*Die Urformen der mobilen Behausung sind die Zelte der Nomadenvölker in den Wüsten Asiens, Nordamerikas und Afrikas. Sie werden heute noch genau wie früher verwendet und unterscheiden sich je nach Einsatzgebiet in Aussehen, Konstruktion und Bezeichnung. Zu den bekanntesten Zeltformen gehören die Jurte, das Tipi und das Schwarzzelt bzw. die Kohte.*

*Ein Haus im „zivilisierten" Verständnis verfügt über Außenmauern, Innenwände und Türen. Die Idee, dieses Wohnmodell von seiner Starrheit zu befreien und es transportfähig zu machen, konkretisiert sich im Fertigbau: Industriell hergestellte Module werden direkt am Aufstellungsort innerhalb kürzester Zeit montiert.*

The first important date in the history of prefabrication was 1848, the year of the California Gold Rush. People arrived from far and wide in need of something more than just the wagons that had brought them there. The material used in prefabricated houses was initially wood, to which steel and aluminum were then added. The continued evolution of the concept then yielded houses and ready-made dwellings that could be transported by land, air or sea. From housing and emergency facilities to shops and schools it is now possible to envision mobile units equipped with every comfort and ready to fulfill nearly any function.

*Die Anfänge der Fertigbauweise gehen auf das Jahr 1848 und den beginnenden kalifornischen Goldrausch zurück: Goldgräber aus aller Welt kommen mit Planwagen, die sie bald durch komfortablere Unterkünfte ersetzen wollen. Diese bestehen anfänglich aus Holz, später werden sie durch die Materialien Stahl und Aluminium ergänzt. Die Entwicklung des Fertigbauverfahrens hat im Lauf der Zeit wichtige Ergebnisse hervorgebracht: komplette Häuser, die mit Lkw, Bahn oder Schiff zu transportieren sind, und bezugsfertig montierte Wohneinheiten, die einfach im Gelände aufgestellt werden können. Von dauerhaften Wohnungen über Notunterkünfte, von Geschäften über Ausstellungspavillons bis hin zu Schulen – heute sieht man für die unterschiedlichsten Zwecke konzipierte Gebäude mit jeglichem Komfort um die Welt reisen.*

Vacations have also been defined by this sense of mobile living, with examples ranging from tents and caravans to motor homes and vacation homes placed in inaccessible locations.

*Homes on the Move* offers a selection of mobile homes that have marked major milestones in the history of design and architecture. Some were chosen for their functionality, some for their sustainability, and others still for their aesthetic appeal. What unites them all, however, is a philosophy in which nothing is fixed and where interiors and exteriors merge.

*Eine weitere typische Situation für das mobile Wohnen – und sei es auch nur für kurze Zeit – ist der Urlaub. Für diesen Zweck sind spezielle Wohnformen entstanden, vom Campingzelt über das Wohnmobil und den Wohnwagen bis hin zum richtigen Haus, die auch in unwegsamen Gegenden, in den Bergen oder direkt am Strand aufgestellt werden können.*

Homes on the Move *versammelt eine Auswahl verschiedener Arten von mobilen Häusern, die als Meilensteine in der Entwicklung des Designs und der Architektur gelten können. Einige wurden wegen ihrer praktischen, andere wegen ihrer ästhetischen Vorzüge ausgewählt, manche aufgrund einer nachhaltigen Bauweise und der Verwendung umweltverträglicher Baumaterialien. Sie alle sind Beispiele für eine Wohnform, bei der nichts starr festgelegt ist und bei der Innen- und Außenraum zu einer Einheit verschmelzen.*

# 1

from the origins to 1960

von den Anfängen bis 1960

## The advent of temporary structures for residential purposes

The history of the tent, home to nomadic peoples and the first example of a temporary dwelling, dates back more than 2,000 years, but it was in the 19th century that we first saw a real proliferation of its uses. A prime example of mobile tents was the wagons used by American pioneers on the long journey out West. The first caravan soon followed, a design officially conceived in 1886 in England by a Dr. Stables.

Design and innovation continued apace into the next century. The first trailer to be towed by vehicles dates back to 1920, and the 1930s saw the birth of the Airstream, an aluminium trailer that has reached cult status in the United States.

The first prefabricated houses were initially experiments, temporary dwellings of spartan design built from whatever materials were available. It was not until 1848 that these abodes were produced on a larger scale, and it wasn't until the first decades of the twentieth century that architects turned their attention toward prefabrication systems, designing structures for residential purposes as well as emergency facilities. Among those who played a crucial role in this development were Le Corbusier and Jean Prouvé of France, Walter Gropius of Germany, and various designers based in North America such as Buckminster Fuller, Frank Lloyd Wright, Richard Neutra, Charles and Ray Eames, and Mies van der Rohe.

The element that unites their work is the concept of employing basic reusable modules that can be expanded as desired. In the 1950s, motorisation and a general acceptance of mobility then engendered a boom in prefabricated housing in the United States.

## Die Anfänge der mobilen, temporären Wohnformen

*Das Zelt als Behausung der Nomadenvölker und Urform provisorischen Wohnens weist eine über 2000-jährige Tradition auf und wird noch heute genutzt. Ab dem 19. Jahrhundert hat es sich jedoch in unterschiedliche Richtungen weiterentwickelt und verbreitet. Ein Beispiel ist der Planwagen, mit dem die nordamerikanischen Pioniere auf der Suche nach neuen Siedlungsgebieten die lange Reise gen Westen antreten. Der erste Wohn-*

*wagen wird offiziell 1886 in England von Dr. Gordon Stables gebaut. 1920 folgen die als Anhänger konzipierten Wohnwagen, die fahrbaren Häusern ähneln. In den 1930er-Jahren wird in den USA der Airstream aus der Taufe gehoben, ein Wohnwagen aus Aluminium.*

*Die ersten Fertighäuser sind zunächst noch Experimente: Spartanisch-provisorische Rückzugsorte, die aus vor Ort gefundenen Materialien zusammengebaut werden. 1848 fängt man an, Fertighäuser in Serie zu produzieren. In den ersten Jahrzehnten des 20. Jahrhunderts beginnen renommierte Architekten mit der Entwicklung von Fertigbausystemen sowohl für Notunterkünfte als auch für herkömmliche Wohnungen, darunter Le Corbusier und Jean Prouvé in Frankreich, Buckminster Fuller, Frank Lloyd Wright, Richard Neutra, Charles und Ray Eames sowie Mies van der Rohe in Amerika und Walter Gropius in Deutschland. Ihre Entwürfe verbindet die Verwendung eines Basismoduls, das theoretisch viele Male wiederholbar ist, sodass das Haus bei Bedarf unproblematisch erweitert werden kann.*

*Der rasche Anstieg der Motorisierung und der Trend zum häufigen Wechsel des Wohnorts führen in den Vereinigten Staaten der 1950er-Jahre zu einem regelrechten Boom der Fertigbauweise.*

**Travelling light in search of a place to stay**

*Unkompliziertes Reisen auf der Suche nach einem Wohnort*

The tent design that is most prevalent in our collective imagination is the Native American tipi of the Great Plains. This mobile abode was easy to erect and dismantle and, most importantly, it was easily transported when tribes needed to follow migrating herds of bison. The tipi has an unmistakable cone shape and its structure consists of braided birch poles leaned together and bound at the top. The design allowed for groundwater run-off and an opening at the apex allowed smoke from the fire to escape. Traditionally, animal hides were used to cover the tipi. This not only made it waterproof but also kept it cool during summer and warm during winter. That technique is still used by some indigenous populations in Canada and Eurasia but most tipis these days are covered with treated canvas.

*Das Tipi ist das Zelt par excellence und wurde ursprünglich von den Urein- wohnern der Great Plains in Nordamerika genutzt. Es ist einfach aufzu- bauen und konnte problemlos mitgenommen werden, wenn der Stamm weiterzog, um den Viehherden zu folgen. Das Zelt besteht aus einem Gestell aus Birkenholzstämmen, die am oberen Ende zusammengebun- den werden, wodurch die charakteristische Kegelform zustande kommt. Dank eines Systems von Öffnungen am unteren Rand und an der Spitze des Tipis kann in seiner Mitte ein Feuer brennen. Die Bespannung aus Tier- häuten ist wasserdicht, schützt im Winter vor schlechtem Wetter und im Sommer vor der Sonneneinstrahlung. Auch heute noch bauen einige Bevölkerungsgruppen in Kanada sowie die Rentierhirten Eurasiens ihre Tipis auf diese Weise. Die eigentlichen Indianer dagegen, die heute in Reservaten leben, verwenden für die Bespannung Leinen.*

Tipi Tents, America

## The archetype of the nomadic dwelling
### *Die traditionelle Nomadenunterkunft*

The Central Asian yurt is one of the first examples of mobile architecture. Its defining characteristic, which makes it ideal for a nomadic lifestyle, is the ease with which it can be assembled and dismantled. The tent is mainly associated with Mongolian culture and its more than 2,000-year-old design is still in use today. It has a circular, self-supporting structure of braided wood and is covered in felts to protect its occupants from the bitter cold winters on the steppe. A wooden ring at the crown of the yurt rests on a pole in the center of the tent to support the ceiling beams. In addition to the wool or felt that covers the floor, interior furnishings may include decorated benches, pillows, a stove, and other survival amenities.

*Das Zelt gilt als klassisches Beispiel der mobilen Behausung: Seine Besonderheit besteht in der Tatsache, dass es einfach ab- und wieder aufzubauen ist und sich somit gut für die nomadische Lebensform eignet. Der Typus der Jurte wird in Zentralasien seit über 2000 Jahren genutzt, vor allem von den Mongolen. Noch heute leben viele Bevölkerungsgruppen in Jurten. Das Aussehen dieser Zelte blieb im Lauf der Jahrhunderte unverändert: Die selbsttragende Konstruktion auf rundem Grundriss besteht aus einem Holzgitter, das zum Schutz vor der Kälte mit Filzdecken verkleidet wird. Ein Holzkreis in der Mitte des Daches stützt die Enden des Gitters und wird von in der Mitte des Zeltes aufgestellten Pfosten gehalten. Die Einrichtung kann neben den Woll- oder Filzteppichen, die den Boden bedecken, verzierte Sitzbänke aus Holz, Kissen, Öfen und alles Weitere umfassen, was man zum Leben braucht.*

**The wait is over for the American dream**
*Der amerikanische Traum kann nicht warten*

In 1868, the great exodus into the American West, the so-called Wild West, had reached its peak. Only the bravest pioneers undertook this dangerous journey, and they did so in large wooden wagons drawn by oxen or horses. The structure was covered by canvas and comfort was sacrificed in order to ensure a lightweight frame. The cover also served as a place to sleep at night and as protection from the elements. The interior was filled with all the amenities and food that the pioneer family would need for the long journey. Always undertaken in caravan with other families, the wagon trains were in motion for up to 18 hours a day, with only the dream of a "promised land" as an incentive for the perilous crossing.

*1868 ist das Jahr der großen Auswanderungswelle in das westliche Nordamerika, den mythischen Wilden Westen. Nur die mutigsten Siedler entschließen sich zu dieser gefährlichen Reise und besteigen große Holzwagen, die von Pferden oder Ochsen gezogen werden. Die Wagen sind lediglich mit einem Kutschbock und einer leichten Leinenplane ausgestattet: Es gilt, das Gewicht möglichst gering zu halten, zulasten der Bequemlichkeit. Der Planwagen wird mit dem Hausrat der Familie und den für die lange Reise notwendigen Lebensmitteln beladen. Die Plane dient zum Schutz in der Nacht, vor Kälte und schlechtem Wetter. Mehrere Familien mit ihren Fuhrwerken bilden jeweils einen Treck und reisen gemeinsam bis zu 18 Stunden am Tag: eine harte Probe, die zu bestehen allein der Traum vom verheißenen Land möglich macht.*

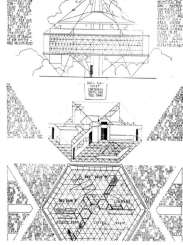

**Suspended house of the future**
*Das Haus der Zukunft in luftiger Höhe*

**Design:** Buckminster Fuller

In 1928, Buckminster Fuller developed a revolutionary "house of the future" concept. The design called for a lightweight, cost-effective and easy-to-build solution to home building. Fuller decided on aluminum to construct the jellyfish-like structure, which was suspended in the air by steel cables attached to a central pylon in order to save ground space. The dome-shaped roof was designed to harness the wind for natural air conditioning, while the transparent walls were made of glass and hard rubber. At that time, bathrooms were often outside the house, so Fuller created instead a plastic module that combined all functionality into the one dwelling. There was also a washing machine, typewriter, telephone, and a television. The house ultimately proved unsuccessful, and Fuller was never able produce it on the scale he had intended.

*1928 entwarf Buckminster Fuller ein Haus der Zukunft, das absolut revolutionär war. Seiner Ansicht nach sollte ein Haus einfach und preisgünstig zu bauen und unkompliziert zu nutzen sein. Deshalb verwendete er als Material für die tragende Struktur Aluminium und hängte den Bau mit Stahlkabeln an einem Pfeiler auf, wodurch zugleich Bauland gespart wurde. Seine Entwurfszeichnungen erinnern entfernt an Quallen. Als Dach entwickelte Fuller eine Kuppelform, um den Wind für die Lüftung auszunutzen. Die transparenten Wände bestanden aus Glas, die Fußböden aus Hartgummi. Das Bad entwarf Fuller aus einem Plastik-Monoblock, der alle Funktionen vereinte. Außerdem verfügte das Haus über eine Waschmaschine, ein Telefon, eine Schreibmaschine und sogar einen Fernseher. Fullers Entwurf blieb erfolglos, weil er – Ironie des Schicksals – zu modern war und niemals in Serie produziert wurde.*

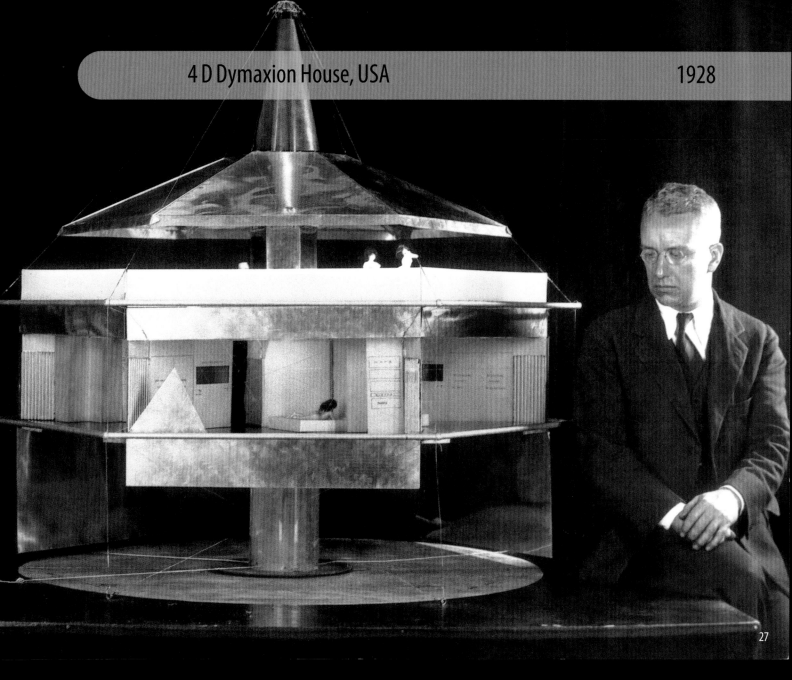

**Lightweight, elegant and innovative**
*Leichtigkeit, Eleganz und Innovation*

**Design:** Wallace Merle "Wally" Byam

Today, it's nothing new to see futuristic mobile homes meandering down the highway, but the tapered design and reflective aluminum of the iconic Airstream trailers never cease to enchant us. Dating back to the 1930's, and still made today, the exterior is much like the fuselage of a plane. The interior, which can accommodate up to four people, was innovative in its use of electric light bulbs for interior lighting and even incorporated an HVAC unit. The standout feature of this trailer, however, is its lightweight aluminum construction – the ultimate image of the Airstream is a photo of French cyclist Latourneau pulling one on his bicycle.

*Zwar sind wir heute den Anblick futuristisch aussehender Wohnwagen auf den Straßen gewohnt, dennoch haben die kultigen Airstream-Modelle aus den 1930er-Jahren, die auch heute noch produziert werden, mit ihrer schlanken, aluminiumglänzenden Karosserie nichts von ihrem Zauber verloren. Ihr Äußeres erinnert an einen Flugzeugrumpf und wurde im Laufe der Jahre nur einer geringfügigen Modellpflege unterzogen, die an der geglückten Designlinie kaum etwas veränderte. Dieser innovative Wohnwagen ist erstmals mit elektrischen Glühbirnen und einer Anlage zur Erwärmung und Abkühlung der Raumluft ausgestattet. Eine weitere Besonderheit des Airstream, der bis zu vier Personen Platz bietet, ist sein geringes Eigengewicht, das er dem Einsatz von Aluminium verdankt. Diesen Aspekt verdeutlicht ein Foto, das den bekannten Radfahrer Latourneau auf dem Fahrrad beim Ziehen eines Airstream zeigt.*

## The symbol of Modernism lives on
### *Das Wiederaufleben eines Symbols der Moderne*

**Design:** Ludwig Mies van der Rohe

Considered one of Mies van der Rohe's most important projects and one of the purest expressions of European Modernism, Farnsworth House's slender lines and geometric design have ensured its position as a national landmark. Located in Illinois, the house is the result of much experimentation and research, and every architectural element has been reduced to its essence. This is exemplified by the load-bearing backbone of the house, whose functional nature also supports an aesthetic component. Completing the structure are lightweight, floor to ceiling windows that take the place of heavy, fixed walls to ensure that natural light floods into the basic open living space, which is accented only by curtains and furniture. The minimalist furnishings were designed by Mies van der Rohe himself and are inspired by the colours of nature.

*Dieses Wohnhaus mit seinen grazilen, geometrischen Formen gilt als einer der wichtigsten Entwürfe von Mies van der Rohe und ein Meisterwerk der europäischen Moderne. Es befindet sich in Illinois, ist Ergebnis einer langen Reihe von Studien und Experimenten und wird heute als Nationalmuseum genutzt. Jedes architektonische Element ist hier auf das Wesentliche reduziert. Die tragende Struktur wird betont und erhält zugleich eine ästhetische Funktion. Fenster ersetzen feste, schwere Wände, sodass die Umgebung das Haus zu durchdringen scheint. Licht erfüllt den offenen Raum, der nur von Einrichtungsgegenständen, den umlaufenden Vorhängen und Drapierungen definiert wird. Mies van der Rohe entwarf selbst die naturfarbenen Möbel, deren Design der minimalistischen Architektur entspricht.*

Transparent architecture dazzles in the desert
*Architektonische Transparenz – eine Oase inmitten der Wüste*

**Design:** Richard Neutra

This oasis of glass, steel, and timber stands in the middle of a California desert landscape. The architecture is characteristic of its designer, Richard Neutra, whose rational approach to the dwelling is visible in both the structure and its furnishings. The frame of the house is steel, while the back wall and one of the side walls are covered in movable steel fins that regulate light and heat inside the living space. The front wall and opposing side are fitted with sliding glass windows that can be fully opened to the elements. The interior is one large space where floor and ceiling are clad with thin wooden facing. Water is another common characteristic in Neutra's projects. At the Kaufmann House, an elegant staircase leads you down to the pool, which is dug in at a lower level to the house.

*Mitten in der kalifornischen Wüste erhebt sich eine Oase aus Glas, Stahl und Holz. Der rationalistische Ansatz der Architektur zeigt sich am gesamten Bauwerk, außen, innen und sogar bei der Einrichtung. Das Stahlskelett reicht bis zum Flachdach hinauf. Ein System aus Stahllamellen, die sich wie Fächer öffnen und den Lichteinfall regeln, schließt die gesamte Rückwand sowie eine Seitenwand ab. Die Front und die andere Seitenwand bestehen dagegen aus gläsernen Schiebetüren und können sich vollständig zur Umgebung hin öffnen. Fußboden und Decke des einzigen großen Innenraums sind mit dünnen Holztafeln verkleidet. Elegante Stufen führen zum Pool hinab, der auf einer tieferen Ebene liegt: Wasser ist ein charakteristisches Element der Architektur von Richard Neutra, selbst dort, wo Wassermangel herrscht.*

**In search of housing for all**
*Auf der Suche nach dem Haus für jedermann*

**Design:** Lustron Corporation

After the Second World War, the desire of builders and architects to design prefabricated houses for everyone was a common goal. During this period Lustron devised an innovative project: a 12-ton prefabricated home, built with steel panels. Sales were achieved through an effective advertising campaign that showed women satisfied with their elegant Lustron Home. This mobile home faithfully reproduces the classic American homestead down to the porch. Fully customizable paint colors ensure that once purchased, the unit is delivered preassembled, on board a truck. Lustron Homes remain inhabited today, however, despite selling 2,500 homes; the price of steel rendered the design unsustainable.

*Nach dem Zweiten Weltkrieg fiel die Idee von Konstrukteuren und Architekten, ein für jedermann erschwingliches Fertighaus zu konzipieren, auf fruchtbaren Boden. Lustron legte in dieser Zeit einen innovativen Entwurf vor: fertige Wohneinheiten aus Stahlplatten mit einem Gesamtgewicht von 12 t. Der Verkauf wurde von einer wirkungsvollen Werbekampagne begleitet, die glückliche und zufriedene Frauen mit ihrem eleganten Lustron Home zeigte. Dieses mobile Haus ist ein getreues Abbild des klassischen amerikanischen Einfamilienhauses mit Dach, Fenstern und Veranda. Nach der Bestellung erreicht es seinen Zielort per Lastwagen in bereits montiertem Zustand. Nichtsdestotrotz kann es individuell gestaltet und gestrichen werden. Allein die übermäßige Verwendung von Stahl treibt den Verkaufspreis allzu sehr in die Höhe. Von den Lustron Homes wurden insgesamt 2500 Modelle veräußert, einige sind noch heute bewohnt.*

# 2

from 1960 to 1980

_____

von 1960 bis 1980

## The economic prosperity of the 1960s gives new meaning to nomadic lifestyles

It was a time when people began moving not out of necessity, but of their own free will. Companies dedicated themselves to creating temporary vacation homes like Casa Minolina 51, a prefabricated abode designed by Giulio Minoletti. At the same time, Volkswagen began producing vehicles like the wildly successful Transporter, a stroke of mobile camping genius. There were also ideas for vacation villages, one example being the lightweight, transportable and futuristic Six-shell-bubble units designed by Jean Benjamin Maneval – a few examples of which have survived to this day.

These were also the years of Buckminster Fuller's geodesic domes (spherical structures suitable as exhibition spaces or temporary dwellings) and projects like the Nakagin Capsule Tower, a fully modular skyscraper designed by Kisho Kurokawa in 1969.

The following decade will be remembered as the most revolutionary with regard to modular design. In 1972, MoMA held an exhibition dedicated to Italian design entitled "Italy: The New Domestic Landscape". Among the most significant projects featured were: Total Furnishing Unit by Joe Colombo, Unità di emergenza FIAT-Anic by Marco Zanuso, and Mobile House by Alberto Roselli and Isao Hosoe.

The 1970s marked an era of experimentation with avant-garde techniques, new materials such as plastic and fiberglass, and with reflection, like Aldo Rossi's Teatro del mondo project, a nod to classical interpretations.

## Wohlstand in den 1960er-Jahren und die Neubewertung des Nomadentums

*Ortswechsel gelten nicht mehr unbedingt als notwendiges Übel, sondern können auch eine willkommene Abwechslung darstellen. Firmen spezialisieren sich auf den Bau temporärer Unterkünfte für die Ferien. Ein Beispiel hierfür ist das von Giulio Minoletti entworfene Fertighaus Casa Minolina 51. Firmen wie Volkswagen produzieren Fahrzeuge, die zu bequemen fahrbaren Unterkünften werden können, wie die VW-Busse, die in der*

*Camper-Version unvergessliche Erfolge feiern. Ganze Feriendörfer entstehen aus leichten, mobilen Wohneinheiten: Bekannt ist in diesem Zusammenhang das futuristische Six-shell-bubble von Jean Benjamin Maneval, von dem heute noch einige Exemplare existieren. Zur selben Zeit entwickelt Buckminster Fuller die geodätischen Kuppeln, kugelförmige Gebilde, die sich besonders als Pavillons oder für temporäre Notunterkünfte eignen. 1969 entsteht der Nagakin Capsule Tower, ein Hochhaus aus austauschbaren Würfeln nach einem Entwurf von Kisho Kurokawa.*

*Das folgende Jahrzehnt bringt hinsichtlich der modularen Architektur eine regelrechte Revolution mit sich. 1972 zeigt das MoMA in New York eine legendäre Ausstellung zum italienischen Design – „Italy: the New Domestic Landscape". Die Total Furnishing Unit von Joe Colombo, die Notunterkunft Fiat-Anic von Marco Zanuso sowie das Mobile House von Alberto Rosselli und Isao Hosoe sind hier an herausragenden Entwürfen vertreten. Es sind die Jahre der avantgardistischen Lösungen und der Experimente mit neuen Materialien wie Plastik und Fiberglas. Manche Architekten finden die Inspirationsquelle für ihre Zukunftsentwürfe auch in den klassischen Formen der Vergangenheit, darunter Aldo Rossi mit seinem Teatro del mondo.*

## Vacation in the natural comfort of a garden house
*Ferien in der Natur in einem komfortablen Gartenhaus*

**Design:** Giulio Minoletti

Inspired by the rational, this prefabricated vacation home designed by Giulio Minoletti experienced great success in the 1960s. Casa Minolina 51 has a very simple and functional structure and reflects its creator's interest in standardising various elements, from the floors to the interior and exterior walls. In doing so, he takes inspiration from traditional Japanese houses. The exterior of the dwelling is covered with panels of steel and glass. Shaped like a parallelogram, it is raised off the ground and is only accessible by ladder. The interior, which measures 44 sq m (473 sq ft) and is divided by movable panels, is clad in warm mahogany. Casa Minolina 51 is equipped with kitchen, bathroom, living room and bedrooms with bunk beds.

*Dieses vom Rationalismus beeinflusste Fertigbauhaus war in den 1960er-Jahren als Feriendomizil ein großer Erfolg. Casa Minolina 51 ist einfach und funktional gestaltet: Giulio Minoletti fasst damit seine Überlegungen zur Standardisierung aller Wohnelemente vom Fußboden bis zu den Innen- und Außenwänden zusammen, ein typisches Charakteristikum beispielsweise japanischer Häuser. Von außen erscheint das Gebäude als langer, mit Stahlblech und Glas verkleideter Quader, der aufgeständert und über eine Treppe zugänglich ist. Bewegliche Wände teilen den 44 m² großen Innenraum in kleinere Bereiche auf, und die Mahagoniverkleidung verleiht ihm die warme Atmosphäre eines „echten" Wohnhauses. Die Ausstattung umfasst Küche, Bad, einen Wohnraum und Schlafzimmer mit Etagenbetten.*

**44**

### The ideal way to tour and vacation
*Das ideale Verkehrsmittel für Urlaub und Tournee*

Design: Volkswagen-Westfalia

The celebrated Volkswagen Transporter van, rolling off the line since 1949. Based on the mechanics of the ever-popular Beetle, and with speeds of nearly 100km/h, this functional and versatile vehicle with the fun and friendly look is at home transporting either cargo or people. The Westfalia version has a kitchen, a bed and built-in cabinets along with a sunroof to ventilate the cabin even when it rains. In the 1960s it became popular among hippies in Europe and America, and produced versions such as the Samba Bus (21-window). Adopted by thousands of families as well as famous bands who took it on tours, the VW bus has long been an ideal way to travel and vacation.

*Diese Campingbus-Variante des bekannten VW-Transporters wurde von Volkswagen ab 1949 produziert: Die Technik ist vom VW-Käfer übernommen, womit der Bus eine Höchstgeschwindigkeit von fast 100 km/h erreicht. Er sieht nett und lustig aus und eignet sich als funktionales, vielseitiges Verkehrsmittel ideal sowohl für den Gütertransport als auch zur Personenbeförderung. Er verfügt über eine Küche, Betten, einen Schrank und ein Bad und kann, dank des Aufstelldachs, auch bei Regen belüftet werden. In den 1960er-Jahren war er das Lieblingsgefährt der Hippies in Europa wie auch in den USA und wurde in den Versionen Samba-Bus (der zweifarbige Kleinbus) und Westfalia (das Wohnmobil) gebaut. Viele berühmte Musikbands nutzten ihn auf der ganzen Welt für ihre Tourneen, und Millionen Familien wählten ihn als ideales Reisemobil für die Ferien.*

## The ufo village
### *Mit Ufos ins Dorf*

**Design:** Jean Benjamin Maneval

In 1968, when the Six-shell-bubble appeared in a Pyrenean vacation village, it was as if UFOs had finally arrived on Earth. In reality, the anomaly was a fully industrialized mobile home project consisting of six fiberglass modules designed for easy assembly and transportability that came in three different colors (green, brown and white) in order to blend in with the landscape. Forty years after its conception, German artist and architect Knitz fell in love with one that had fallen into disuse and decided to buy it. Today you can admire it in the backyard of Knitz's house in Ravensburg where it is used as a studio and enjoyed as a symbol of the visionary projects of the 1960s.

*Als die Six-shell-bubble 1968 in einem französischen Feriendorf in den Pyrenäen auftauchten, dachte so mancher an die Landung von Raumkapseln auf der Erde. In Wirklichkeit handelte es sich um eine mobile, vollständig industriell hergestellte Architektur. Jeweils sechs Zellen aus Fiberglas bilden zusammen eine einheitliche Struktur, die für den raschen Aufbau und Transport konzipiert wurde. Für eine optimale Integration in die Landschaft waren sie in drei verschiedenen Farben erhältlich: Grün, Braun und Weiß. Vierzig Jahre später verliebt sich der deutsche Künstler und Architekt Knitz in eine der ausrangierten Zellen und beschließt, sie zu kaufen. Heute kann sie im Hof seines Hauses in Ravensburg besichtigt werden. Sie dient ihm als Architekturbüro und erinnert an die „visionären" Projekte der 1960er-Jahre.*

# 50

**The stand-alone bubble**
*Eine große Kugel trägt sich selbst*

**Design:** Buckminster Fuller

Montreal's Geodesic Dome, which takes its name from the mathematical term meaning the shortest path between two points within a sphere, was built as the pavilion for the United States Expo in 1967. Its structure was formed by a honeycombed steel lattice with cells covered in acrylic. The interior was designed over seven levels and divided into four thematic areas. It even had a 37-m-high (121-ft) elevator. In 1976 a fire destroyed the acrylic cells but the steel frame is still standing. Today, as the Biosphère, its grandeur and transparency continue to fascinate, only now as a museum dedicated to the environment.

*Die Bezeichnung „geodätische Kuppel" geht auf das mathematische Konzept der Geodätik zurück: Die geodätische Linie beschreibt die kürzeste Verbindungslinie zwischen zwei Punkten – im Fall der Kugeloberfläche stets eine Kurve mit demselben Durchmesser wie die Kugel selbst. Der Geodesic Dome wurde als amerikanischer Pavillon anlässlich der Weltausstellung von 1967 in Montreal errichtet. Er besteht aus einem Stahlnetz und Waben aus Acrylglas und war in sieben Ebenen mit vier thematischen Bereichen unterteilt. Sogar eine Rolltreppe wurde gebaut, die eine Höhe von 37 m erreichte – für die damalige Zeit ein absoluter Rekord. Ein Feuer zerstörte 1976 die Acrylwaben, nicht aber das Stahlnetz, das noch original erhalten ist. Heute heißt es „Biosphère", beeindruckt noch immer durch seine Größe und Transparenz und beherbergt ein Umweltmuseum.*

## The capsule skyscraper
### *Der Wolkenkratzer im Karton*

**Design:** Kisho Kurokawa

The Nakagin Capsule Tower represented a concept of modern living in Japan in the 1970s and was the first example of multimodular, prefabricated architecture to be applied to a larger building in an urban setting. Each unit in the building looks like a space capsule and is designed to be repositioned or changed depending on its use. The living cells are preassembled at the factory with all the furniture, equipment and technology, and can be configured to your needs. Each unit measures 10 sq m (107 sq ft), has porthole windows and is delivered complete with bedroom, bathroom and accessories such as a TV, radio and an alarm clock. The project has become a symbol of interchangeable, recyclable and sustainable architecture.

*Der Nakagin Capsule Tower gilt als erstes Beispiel einer variablen Fertigbauarchitektur in großem Maßstab für ein städtisches Umfeld und reflektiert das moderne Lebensgefühl der 1970er-Jahre in Japan. Jede einzelne Wohneinheit kann je nach Bedarf positioniert und verändert werden. Die Wohnzellen, die von innen wie Raumkapseln aussehen, werden an der Produktionsstätte samt Möbeln und technischer Ausstattung vormontiert. Die Innenräume können nach der Montage den eigenen Vorstellungen entsprechend angepasst werden. Jede Einheit ist etwa 10 m² groß, hat ein Bullauge als Fenster und wird komplett mit Schlafzimmer, Bad und Zubehör wie Fernseher, Radio und Wecker ausgeliefert. Dieses Gebäude ist zum Symbol und Wegbereiter einer nachhaltigen, veränderbaren und recyclingfähigen Architektur geworden.*

Nakagin Capsule Tower, Japan          1969–1972

**A mobile house that opens and shuts like a box**

*Ein mobiles Haus, das sich wie eine Schachtel öffnen und schließen lässt*

**Design:** Marco Zanuso

The concept of a prefabricated mobile module is applied to this emergency unit as well. Given the nature of the challenge, the first problem Marco Zanuso had to face was the logistical issue of creating a compact structure that could be easily transported and ready for use at a disaster site. The solution was highly functional: transportable on a flatbed, enclosed on all sides and, once positioned on the ground, boxed modules extend on platforms from the container itself. The wood-paneled interior can thus be doubled in size with all the amenities of a static home: kitchen, bathroom, bedroom and a connection to the power grid.

*Mit dieser Notunterkunft erobert die Fertigbauweise die „mobile Kapsel". Die primäre Herausforderung, der sich Marco Zanuso zu stellen hatte, betraf Transport- und Logistikfragen: Die Aufgabe verlangte eine kompakte, leicht aufbaubare Architektur, die einfach zu befördern war und bei einer Katastrophe sofort zur Verfügung stand. Das Ergebnis war ein Container, der während des Lkw-Transports zunächst allseitig geschlossen bleibt. Am Aufstellungsort zieht man die bewohnbaren Kuben heraus, die auf ebenfalls ausziehbaren Plattformen aufliegen. Die Zimmer wachsen also gleichsam wie magische Schachteln aus dem Container heraus, wobei sich die Fläche verdoppelt und der Raum komfortabel wird. Er verfügt über holzverkleidete Wände und Teppichböden und ist auch sonst wie ein richtiges Wohnhaus ausgestattet: Es gibt eine Küche, ein Bad, ein Schlafzimmer und Anschlüsse für die Energieversorgung.*

# 58

## When space is not enough
### *Wenn der Raum nicht ausreicht*

**Design:** Alberto Rosselli, Isao Hosoe

Two principles underscore the design of this mobile home: mobility and expandability. The basic unit measures just 10 sq m (107 sq ft), but can be expanded to nearly triple that area. The long walls can be moved in all directions along telescopic rails and the short walls are expandable too. You can also open the front wall to create a veranda. Only two people are needed to make the changes, and no special equipment is required. The interior, designed for a maximum of six people, is equipped with kitchen, bathroom, sleeping quarters and a living area illuminated by Plexiglass portholes in the roof. Despite a box-like appearance, Mobile House opens out to nature like a blossoming flower.

*Dieses mobile Haus beruht auf zwei Prinzipien: Mobilität und Erweiterung. Die Basiseinheit misst nur 10 m², kann ihre eigentliche Fläche jedoch verdreifachen. Die Wände verlaufen in allen vier Richtungen auf Teleskopschienen. Die langen Seiten des Containers können nach einem Blasebalgsystem aufgefaltet werden, die vordere Wand lässt sich zusätzlich zu einer Veranda öffnen, und auch die kurzen Seiten sind erweiterbar. Den Aufbau können zwei Personen vornehmen, ohne dafür besondere Geräte zu benötigen. Der Wohnraum ist für maximal sechs Personen konzipiert und verfügt über Küche, Bad, Schlaf- und Wohnbereich. Ein rundes, zu öffnendes Plexiglasfenster an der Decke lässt das Tageslicht herein. Hier wohnt es sich wie in einer Schachtel, die sich unversehens – wie eine Blume – zur umgebenden Natur hin öffnet.*

**Functional caravan with veranda**
*Rationalistischer Wohnwagen mit Veranda*

Design: Nizzoli Sistemi (G. Mario Oliveri, Giusi Giuliani,
Roberto Ingegnere, Enrico Picciani)

Until the 1970s, caravans were characterised by the more rounded American designs. The inspiration at Nizzoli studios was to design a mobile home with a streamline form and maximised interior space, the result of which was a more rectangular chassis. The interior aesthetic wasn't the only change. The new design simplified production and reduced construction costs, and made the inclusion of furniture much easier. Caravan Laverda is equipped with a large, aerodynamic window, an expandable rear end that creates another 4 m (13 ft) of usable space and has a cotton tent to create a veranda. The outer body is a pale shade of blue, which blends well with nature.

*Bis in die 1960er-Jahre hinein hatten Wohnwagen im Allgemeinen abgerundete Formen, wie es in Amerika üblich war. Das Ziel von Studio Nizzoli bestand in dem Entwurf eines Modells, das den Innenraum bestmöglich ausnutzt und rationalisiert. Die Folge war eine Weiterentwicklung der Karosserie hin zu einer kantigen Form. Die Neuerungen betrafen jedoch nicht nur die Ästhetik: Die vereinfachte Montage der Innenausstattung erleichterte auch den Produktionsprozess und senkte damit die Konstruktionskosten. Ein großes Panoramafenster erfüllt gleichzeitig eine aerodynamische Funktion. Hinten kann die nutzbare Fläche um 4 m² vergrößert werden, indem ein Verdeck eine zusätzliche Veranda schafft. Durch die hellblaue Karosserie integriert sich der Wohnwagen bestens in die Landschaft.*

## 64

**Prefab on a precipice**
*Ein Fertighaus am Steilhang*

**Design:** Helmut C. Schulitz

When German architect Helmut C. Schulitz moved to California in the 1970s, his research focused on prefabricated structures. At the University of California at Los Angeles, he developed a workshop called T.E.S.T. (Team for Experimental Systems-building Techniques), the scope of which was to create a construction method based around the use of standard prefabricated materials. House in Beverly Hills was the first application of this. Perched on a cliff, the steel and glass modules are anchored to the ground and appear to simply cling to each other. Access to the dwelling is through the dining room, which flows out onto the panoramic terrace that seems to float over the precipice. The bedrooms are downstairs. Perfectly integrated with nature, the scenic impact of this home is impressive.

*1970 zieht der deutsche Architekt Helmut C. Schulitz nach Kalifornien, wo er sich vorwiegend der Fertigbauweise widmet. An der University of California in Los Angeles organisiert er unter dem Titel T.E.S.T. (Team for Experimental Systems-Building Techniques) einen Workshop mit dem Ziel, eine Baumethode auf der Grundlage standardisierter Fertigbauteile und Materialien zu entwickeln. Das Haus in Beverly Hills stellt die erste Anwendung seiner Theorien dar. Es wird an einem Steilhang errichtet: Die Stahl- und Glasmodule sind im Gelände verankert und scheinen sich angesichts des Abgrunds geradezu aneinanderzuklammern. Beim Betreten des Hauses gelangt man in den Essbereich, von wo aus man den Wohnraum sowie die schwebende Panoramaterrasse erreicht. Im Stockwerk darunter befinden sich die verschiedenen Zimmer. Die Wirkung dieses perfekt in die Natur integrierten Hauses ist spektakulär.*

# 68

**Floating theatre**
*Ein schwimmendes Theater*

**Design:** Aldo Rossi

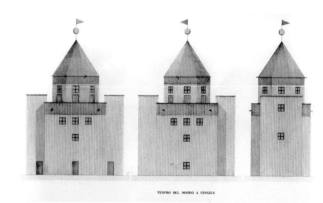

TEATRO DEL MONDO A VENEZIA

One of Aldo Rossi's most fascinating works is this mobile unit that traveled the Venetian canals in 1979–80 for the "Venice Biennale". Built in the local shipyard with traditional materials, this floating theater has a tubular steel frame concealed by wooden cladding. The stage is rectangular, positioned between two opposing platforms, while the galleries are spread over three floors, the top one with access to the balcony. Windows throughout the structure allow the spectator to follow the show and admire the scenery outside at the same time. Inspired by the floating theatres that paraded through Venice from the 16th to the 18th century, its design includes many elements drawn from historical architecture, a common theme in Rossi's work.

*Die mobile Architektur, die 1979 durch Venedigs Kanäle trieb, ist eines der faszinierendsten Werke von Aldo Rossi. Das schwimmende Theater, in dessen Innerem sich ein Vorstellungssaal befindet, wurde in einer Werft gebaut. Verwendet wurden schiffsübliche Materialien, und so verbirgt sich unter der Holzverkleidung ein Gerüst aus Eisenrohren. Die rechteckige Bühne liegt zwischen zwei einander gegenüberliegenden stufenförmigen Rängen. Die Sitzplätze verteilen sich auf drei Blöcke, vom obersten aus betritt man die Aussichtsterrasse. Der Besucher kann das Theaterstück verfolgen und gleichzeitig durch die Fenster auf die Landschaft blicken. Das Teatro del mondo ist von den schwimmenden Theatern im Venedig des 16. und 17. Jahrhunderts inspiriert, seine Gestalt erinnert an geometrische Grundformen (wie den Kegel) und andere wiederkehrende Elemente der Architekturgeschichte, auf die Rossi in seinem Werk gern zurückgreift.*

# 3

from 1980 to 2000

---

von 1980 bis 2000

## The 1980s see a return to the rationalism of the 1920s

Inspired by the great masters, a search began in the 1980s for a better understanding of the notion of habitation. Out of this grew a desire to provide easily accessible solutions for a modern society.

For some architects, notably Helmut C. Schulitz, housing needed to be industrialised and built from standard, easily-assembled components available in a catalogue. The preferred materials during this period were steel and glass, chosen for their durability and modularity. Glass enabled elegant structures to be created and opened a dialogue between buildings and their surroundings.

The search for mass production ultimately placed a great deal of emphasis on the shipping container, a cheap and easy unit to transport by road, rail or ship.

The idea of mobile structures has since captured the imagination of big business, too. Projects like Jean Nouvel's Camion Inox for Sovam Industries and Renzo Piano's Paglione IBM have produced revolutionary projects that are unique to their genre.

The contribution played by artists is also interesting. Fascinated by the potential of mobile architecture, for example, the Van Lieshout Studio developed a traveling museum. During the 1990s, an increasingly popular theme was the sensibility to ecological issues, which became more pronounced with the dawn of the new millennium. Michael Jantzen was one of the protagonists who helped opened the door to environmentally-friendly solutions.

## Die Rückkehr zum Rationalismus der 1920er-Jahre in der mobilen Architektur der 1980er-Jahre

*Unter dem Einfluss der großen Meister beginnt die Suche nach neuen Wohnkonzepten, die auf die Bedürfnisse der modernen Gesellschaft zugeschnitten sind und unkomplizierte, praktische Lösungen bieten. Für einige Architekten, darunter Helmut C. Schulitz, soll die Wohneinheit aus industriell gefertigten, aus dem Katalog bestellbaren und einfach zu montierenden Standardelementen bestehen. In den 1980er-Jahren werden die Materialien Stahl und Glas wegen ihrer Widerstandsfähigkeit und Eignung für modulare Bauweisen bevorzugt. Sie ermöglichen Entwürfe mit eleganten Strukturen, die eine Verbindung zwischen Innen- und Außenraum fördern.*

*Die Frage nach der Serialität findet ihre Antwort in der Verwendung des Containers als Wohneinheit: Er wird industriell hergestellt, kostet nicht viel und kann einfach auf der Straße, auf Schienen oder auf dem Wasser transportiert werden.*

*Die Idee des mobilen Hauses erreicht auch große Unternehmen: So entstehen revolutionäre, einzigartige Bauten wie der Camion Inox von Jean Nouvel für Sovam und der IBM-Pavillon von Renzo Piano.*

*Interessant sind auch die Beiträge von Künstlern, die von den Möglichkeiten der mobilen Architektur fasziniert sind, darunter das Atelier Van Lieshout mit seinen reisenden Museen.*

*In den 1990er-Jahren ist eine wachsende Sensibilität der Planer für Fragen des Umweltschutzes zu beobachten, die Anfang des neuen Jahrtausends bestimmend wird: Michael Jantzen gehört zu den Wegbereitern umweltgerechter Lösungen.*

## Shafts of light define a home
### *Licht gestaltet den Raum*

**Design:** Shoei Yoh

This steel house was designed for a family in Nagasaki that required privacy but didn't want to compromise on light. A decision was thus made to create a building that alternated open and closed spaces. The house was created from a basic module, repeated throughout the structure, and the alternating opaque and transparent forms are visible on both the walls and roof. The design ensures a delightful play of sunlight and shadow inside and a cross-linked light shaft illuminates the floor and minimal furnishings. The slow and steady transition conveys a sense of continuous change. Movable panels divide up the interior and individual rooms depending on the desires or needs of the occupant.

*Dieses Haus aus Stahl wurde für eine Familie aus Nagasaki entworfen, die sich eine geschützte Privatsphäre, zugleich aber auch viel Licht und eine Verbindung zur Außenwelt wünschte. Die Entscheidung fiel auf einen Entwurf, bei dem sich offene und geschlossene Bereiche abwechseln. Er geht von einem Grundmodul aus, das sich am gesamten Bau permanent wiederholt. Der Wechsel von transparenten und lichtundurchlässigen Modulen ist sowohl beim Dach als auch an den Seitenwänden deutlich sichtbar. Im Inneren ruft der Sonneneinfall ein faszinierendes Spiel von Licht und Schatten hervor: Ein zartes Gitternetz zeichnet sich auf dem Fußboden und der minimalistischen Einrichtung ab und vermittelt den Eindruck ständiger Veränderung. Verschiebbare Wände unterteilen den Raum je nach den momentanen Erfordernissen in einzelne Zimmer.*

**Catalogue construction**
*Bauen nach Katalog*

**Design:** Helmut C. Schulitz

Perched up in the Santa Monica Mountains in southern California are the Hollywood Houses, a perfect example of how using prefabricated industrial materials can result in a high-impact architectural aesthetic. Hollywood Houses were designed by Helmut Schulitz according to his TEST (Team for Experimental Systems-Building Techniques) philosophy. The building exclusively uses standard-sized modules and panels from a catalogue. Nothing in these buildings is customised. Steel and glass clad the exterior while wood lines the spacious interior with its comfortable living quarters and bedrooms. The houses are accessed via stairs and exterior corridors, and the top floor offers a breathtaking view of the Los Angeles area and the Pacific Ocean.

*Die Hollywood Houses in den Hügeln von Santa Monica, Kalifornien, sind perfekte Beispiele für eine Fertigbauarchitektur, die hohe ästhetische Ansprüche erfüllt. Der Architekt Helmut Schulitz entwarf sie auf Grundlage des von ihm entwickelten Bausystems T.E.S.T. (Team for Experimental Systems-Building Techniques), das ausschließlich vorfabrizierte Module in Standardmaßen verwendet, die anhand eines Katalogs zusammengestellt werden können. Nichts an diesen Häusern wird also individuell angefertigt. Stahl und Glas für die Außenverkleidungen und Holz für die Fußböden sind die bevorzugten Materialien. Im geräumigen Inneren befinden sich Wohn- und Versorgungsbereiche sowie Schlafzimmer. Der Zugang erfolgt über Außentreppen und Flure. Vom obersten Stockwerk aus bietet sich ein atemberaubender Blick über die Hügel von Los Angeles und den Pazifik.*

An economical house for any emergency
*Das ökonomische Haus für jeden Zweck*

**Design:** Sean Godsell Architects

"You can have a house for the same price as a car," declares Australian architect Sean Godsell. Sensitive to the problem of displaced peoples, his solution to this predicament is Future Shack, a small house built from a steel container 22 ft long that sells for just $30,000. The shipping container, an industrial product that is both modular and durable, guarantees comfort at a low price. The units are easily transported by road, rail or sea and can be assembled in just 24 hours. The module is equipped with solar panels on the gabled roof and telescopic legs that stabilize the module on the ground. The interior is fitted with a kitchen, bathroom and foldaway furniture.

*Ein Haus muss nicht unbedingt mehr kosten als ein Auto: Das behauptet zumindest der australische Architekt Sean Godsell, der sich intensiv mit dem Wohnen unter schwierigen sozialen Bedingungen auseinandergesetzt hat. Sein Vorschlag ist der Future Shack, eine kleine Wohnung, bestehend aus einem etwa 6 m langen Stahlcontainer, der bereits für 30 000 Dollar zu haben ist. Als modulares, langlebiges Industrieprodukt garantiert der Container Komfort zum günstigen Preis. Außerdem lässt sich sein Standort leicht verändern, er reist auf der Straße, mit dem Schiff oder per Bahn. Future Shack ist in 24 Stunden aufgebaut und macht sich je nach Lebenslage als Notunterkunft oder auch als Ferienhaus nützlich. Das Modul verfügt über ein Dach mit Solarzellen und über höhenverstellbare Beine, die für die nötige Stabilität im Gelände sorgen. Im Inneren gibt es eine Küche, ein Bad und versenkbares Mobiliar.*

## A house that opens like a fan
### *Ein fächerartig ausklappbares Wohnmobil*

**Design:** Eduard Böhtlingk

"Markies," meaning veranda in Dutch, is a mobile home designed for the 1986 Temporary Living competition. Its name derives from the fact that when parked, both its walls can be opened electronically like a fan, tripling the size of usable space and creating two wings for living and sleeping. The awning over the living area is transparent PVC while the sleeping quarters are covered with an opaque fabric. Both hoods are adjustable, enabling you to decide whether to close yourself in or open the trailer up to circulate air. The interior is equipped with every comfort: permanent kitchen and bathroom and movable table, benches and bed. Markies won the 1996 Public Prize at the major national design biennial, The Rotterdam Prize.

*Markies, holländisch für „Veranda", ist ein Wohnwagen, der 1986 für den Wettbewerb „Temporary Living" konzipiert wurde. Seinen Namen verdankt er der Tatsache, dass sich seine Wände im Ruhezustand elektronisch wie zwei Flügel nach außen öffnen lassen: Dadurch verdreifacht sich seine Nutzfläche, und zwei Veranden entstehen, eine für die Nacht, eine für den Tag. Der Nachtflügel besteht aus lichtundurchlässigem Stoff, der Tagflügel aus transparentem PVC. Beide Verdecke sind verstellbar – man kann sie sowohl vollständig schließen als auch anheben, etwa zum Lüften. Innen verfügen sie über jeglichen Komfort. Küche und Bad sind fest installierte Bereiche, während sich Tisch, Sitzbänke und Bett versenken lassen und bei Öffnung der Veranden ausgezogen werden können. Markies wurde 1996 beim „Rotterdam Design Prize", einer wichtigen nationalen Design-Biennale, mit dem Publikumspreis ausgezeichnet.*

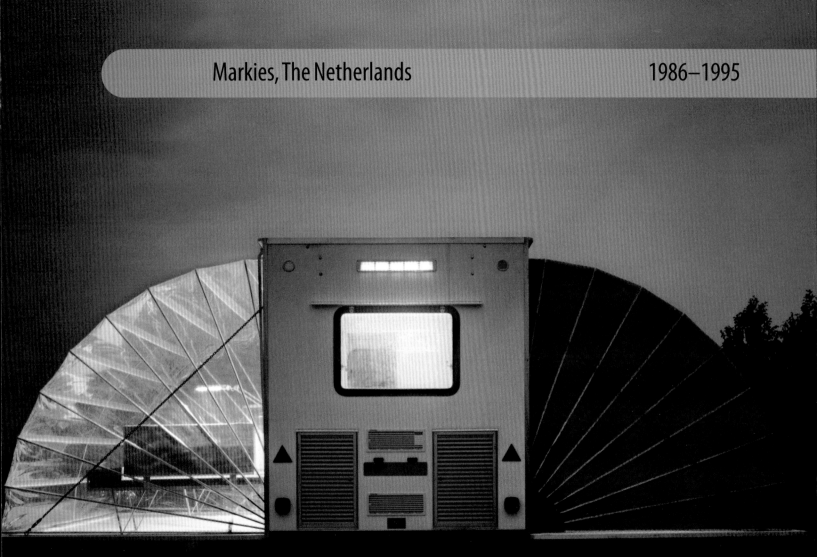

**Two structures – One unique dwelling**
*Zwei Häuser für ein einzigartiges Wohnen*

**Design:** Studio Granda

Two modules with the evocative names House of Delia and House of Saturn make up the Aktion Poliphile house. The architects that designed the house did so with the intention of expressing the opposites that co-exist in humans and in modern society. As such, the two buildings communicate with each other. The House of Saturn, which is reserved for guests, is a rigid and fixed structure with lead tiles on the roof and a warm red tone on windowless walls. The House of Delia, the prefabricated core, is the light and airy image of contemporary living built from cedar wood and steel. A large roof terrace offers a panoramic view of the verdant surroundings.

*Aktion Poliphile, das sind zwei Wohnhäuser mit bezeichnenden Namen: „House of Delia" und „House of Saturn". Mit diesen Entwürfen möchten die Architekten die Gegensätze zum Ausdruck bringen, die den Menschen und die moderne Gesellschaft prägen. Das Gästehaus Saturn hat eine feste und solide Struktur mit einem undurchdringlichen Dach aus Blei. Die in warmem Rot gehaltenen Wände sind kaum durchfenstert. Ganz anders das Haupthaus Delia – mit seiner Leichtigkeit und Modernität ist es ein Spiegelbild des zeitgenössischen Lebens. Fertigbauteile aus Zedernholz und Stahl umspielen hier die Fensterflächen, und von der großzügigen Dachterrasse aus bietet sich ein wunderbarer Blick auf das umgebende Grün. Die beiden Häuser kommunizieren miteinander: Saturns Wände lösen sich gleichsam in Delia auf, und das kräftige Rot des Verputzes geht über in den natürlichen Holzton, der frisch und jung erscheint.*

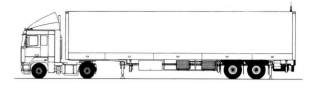

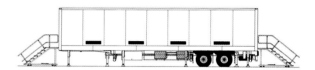

**Art meets industry**
*Die Kunst begegnet der Industrie*

**Design:** Jean Nouvel, Emmanuel Cattani & Associés

The Inox multimedia truck is longer than a regular lorry by 13 m (42 ft) and was born from the idea of creating a traveling space where service industry artists and designers could meet with managers and executives. Once it is opened and expanded it becomes a huge rectangular block of 300 sq m (3,229 sq ft). The project was commissioned to French architect Jean Nouvel by airport facilities manufacturer Sovam. The body is made of stainless steel, a nod to the world of aviation, and the interior space is multifaceted, able to adapt to a variety of activities such as meetings, conferences and art exhibitions. The decor is minimal, with tables, desks and a bar, and the technology inside is nothing less than state of the art.

*Inox ist ein multimedialer Lastwagen. Seine Entstehung beruhte auf der Idee, einen fahrbaren Raum für Begegnungen von Kunst und Unternehmen zu schaffen, in dem sich Künstler und Designer im Dienst der Industrie mit Managern und Führungskräften austauschen können. Mit der Planung des Camion Inox beauftragte Sovam, eine auf die Ausstattung von Flughäfen spezialisierte Firma, den französischen Architekten Jean Nouvel. Es entstand ein typischer Lkw von über 13 m Länge, der sich im Ruhezustand zu einem Parallelepiped mit einer Grundfläche von 300 m² öffnen lässt. Seine Karosserie aus rostfreiem Stahl erinnert an die Welt der Luftfahrt. Der dynamische Innenraum passt sich den vielfältigen Nutzungsmöglichkeiten an: Meetings, Vorträge, Kunstausstellungen. Die reduzierte Innenarchitektur mit Konferenz- und Schreibtischen, Bars und Empfangsbereichen verfügt über eine Hightechausstattung.*

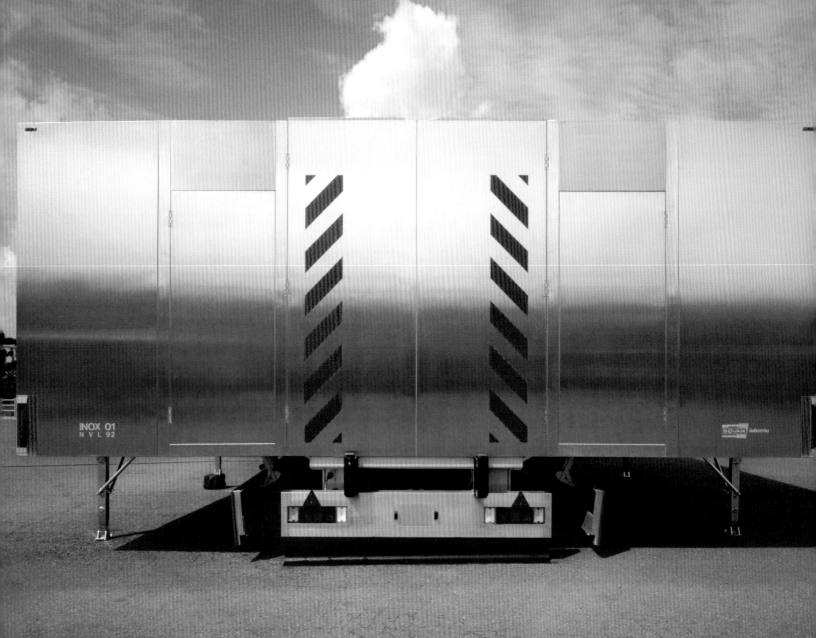

### Life between the Earth and sky
*Wohnen zwischen Himmel und Erde*

**Design:** Shoei Yoh

This glass house built between the sea and the sky appears suspended on a 140-m (460-ft) cliff. The terrace facing the ocean is supported by a steel cantilever and lined with white marble. The façade, subjected to strong winds and salt, offers protection with nothing more than glass panels bonded with silicone. The structure is built with fixed elements and floating panels that let in plentiful light. The interior is dominated by the effects of this light, which in turn merges with the seascape below. This example of refined simplicity, typical of the best Japanese design, reinforces the idea that to live in a glass house is to live in harmony with nature. Although conceived decades ago, Glass House between Sea and Sky is still an important contemporary architectural work.

*Das Glass House scheint zwischen Himmel und Meer über einem 140 m hohen Felsen zu schweben. Seine weit auskragende, mit Marmor verkleidete Stahlterrasse öffnet sich zum Meer. Glasplatten, die nur mit Silikon befestigt sind, schützen die Fassade vor starken Winden und dem Salzgehalt der Luft. Das Haus hat sowohl feststehende als auch bewegliche Elemente wie die großen Glaswände. Ihnen ist es zu verdanken, dass der Innenraum buchstäblich von den Lichtspielen lebt, die wiederum mit der Meereslandschaft verschmelzen. Wer in einem Gebäude aus Glas lebt, geht eine Symbiose mit der Natur ein, nimmt das Rauschen des Meeres und seine langen Ruhephasen wahr: Dieses Haus, das vor 20 Jahren entworfen wurde, ist ein Beispiel für die vornehme Schlichtheit als Kennzeichen eines vollendeten japanischen Stils. Es gilt noch heute als ein bedeutender Entwurf zeitgenössischer Architektur.*

Glass House between Sea and Sky, Japan                    1991

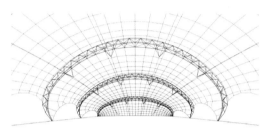

**Commercial marquees**
*Spannkonstruktion für Forschungszwecke*

**Design:** Philippe Samyn & Partners, architects & engineers

Commissioned by industrial chemicals firm Sinco Engineering, M&G is a 3,000-sq-m (32,391-sq-ft) research facility housing a series of offices, design spaces and laboratories. The minimalist yet functional structure is covered by a polyester PVC roof and supported by a spine of six symmetrical steel arches. Other arches at its base follow the perimeter and allow light to enter through transparent plastic panels. M&G Research is positioned at the center of an artificial lake and the soft lines of its elliptical shape mirror the hilly landscape of Venafro in central Italy. The white roof enhances the dramatic nature of the work, a perfect harmony between high technology and natural environment.

*M&G ist tatsächlich ein als Spannkonstruktion gebautes Forschungszentrum. Es wurde vom Chemieunternehmen Sinco Engineering in Auftrag gegeben, ist fast 3000 m² groß und beherbergt in seinem Inneren Büros, Labors sowie Räume mit minimalem, funktionalem Design. Sein Dach besteht aus PVC-beschichtetem Polyester und wird von einem leichten Gerüst aus sechs symmetrisch angeordneten Stahlbögen getragen. An seiner Basis verlaufen weitere Bögen um das gesamte Gebäude herum und lassen durch transparente Kunststofffenster Licht eintreten. M&G Ricerche steht inmitten eines Wasserbeckens und integriert sich dank der weichen Linien seiner elliptischen Form vollkommen in die Hügellandschaft des mittelitalienischen Venafro. Das Weiß der Membran unterstreicht den beeindruckenden Auftritt des Bauwerks: Hightech und Natur in perfekter Harmonie.*

## Architecture and nature become one
*Ein Haus folgt dem Rhythmus der Natur*

**Design:** Lacaton & Vassal

The beautiful plot chosen for this house was covered by trees and mimosa shrubs that sloped down toward the ocean. The task for the architects was therefore to create a building that could be seamlessly incorporated into its surroundings. The solution was an elevated structure on steel pylons that allowed for the key characteristic of the building: the variable height of the first floor, which also allows access to the ground below. The walls of the structure are covered with aluminum sheets, which help increase space and light within the house. Architecture and nature become one in this abode, where even the trees are integrated into the very structure of the building and a large window allows you to take in the beautiful seascape.

*Die passende Naturkulisse für dieses Haus wäre ein charmantes, mit Bäumen und Mimosen bedecktes Grundstück gewesen, das zum Meer hin abfällt. Die Architekten wollten ein Gebäude realisieren, das sich seiner Umgebung weitestgehend anpasst, und wählten eine aufgeständerte Bauweise mit Stahlträgern. Eine Besonderheit ist die variable Höhe des ersten Stockwerks, die einen Durchgang unter dem Haus ermöglicht. Architektur und Natur werden eins: Die Bäume sind in die Gebäudestruktur einbezogen, und eine große Fensterfront gibt den Blick auf ein wunderbares Meerespanorama frei. Die Wände und das Dach sind mit gewelltem Aluminium verkleidet, das den Raum durch Lichtreflexion optisch vergrößert und ihn heller wirken lässt.*

Maison à Lège, Cap Ferret, France 1995–1998

**Modularity meets mobility**
*Mobilität trifft auf Modularität*

**Design:** Atelier Van Lieshout

Similar to an RV, Modular House Mobile is a mobile home characterized by a seemingly unique internal layout. The structure consists of three sections: mechanical, with the cab and chassis; functional, with a kitchen and shower that include hot and cold water; and sleeping quarters. The entire space is itself a psychological study in which different colors demarcate the various interior spaces: red for the sleeping quarters, for example, and shades of white that turn to yellows and browns in the living space. The tactile furnishings include benches and a writing table and the floors are covered in rugs and animal skins.

*Ähnlich einem Wohnmobil, ist das Modular House Mobile ein fahrbares Haus mit einer originellen Innenraumaufteilung. Die Aufmerksamkeit der Planer galt dabei der menschlichen Psychologie: Die Begrenzung der verschiedenen Bereiche ist ganz der Farbgebung überlassen, und auch dank der gewählten Materialien sind hier vielfältige visuelle und taktile Erlebnisse möglich. Der dreiteilige Aufbau besteht aus einem mechanischen Teil mit Fahrerkabine und Fahrgestell, einem Funktionsteil mit Küchen- und Schlafzone, in dem die Farbe Rot vorherrscht, und einem Wohnbereich, der sich auch zum Arbeiten eignet und in dem Weiß in Gelb- und Brauntöne übergeht. Hier gibt es einen Tisch mit Sitzbänken, ein Schreibmöbel, ferner Bad und Dusche mit warmem und kaltem Wasser. Der Fußboden und teilweise auch die Ausstattung sind mit Teppichen und verschiedenen Lederarten verkleidet.*

## Modular House Mobile, The Netherlands 1995

**A vast tensile structure to celebrate the new millenium**
*Eine riesige Spannkonstruktion zur Feier des neuen Jahrtausends*

**Design:** Richard Rogers Partnership

The Millennium Dome, on the banks of the Thames at Greenwich, is the largest covered building in the world. The huge tensile structure made of Teflon-coated fiberglass rises 100 m (328 ft) over London and covers an area of 100,000 sq m (over one million sq ft). Built to celebrate the new millennium at the end of 1999, it is a high-impact architectural structure supported by hundreds of steel rods and poles. It hosted a series of events throughout 2000 and, after a period of closure, was reopened in 2005 as the O2 to house all manner of exhibitions, shows and concerts.

*Der Millennium Dome ist der größte überdachte Baukörper der Welt. Er erhebt sich auf der Halbinsel Greenwich an den Ufern der Themse und bedeckt eine Fläche von mehr als 100 000 m². Die enorme Spannkonstruktion aus teflonbeschichtetem Fiberglas wird von Tausenden von Zugstangen und turmartigen, über 100 m hohen Stahlmasten gehalten. Das Ergebnis ist ein wahres architektonisches Meisterwerk mit großer szenischer Wirkung. Erbaut, um das neue Jahrtausend zu feiern, fanden hier während des Jahres 2000 zahlreiche Events und Ausstellungen statt. Nach einer längeren Schließphase dient es heute unter dem neuen Namen O2 mit Bars, Restaurants, Kinos und Ausstellungsbereichen der Freizeitgestaltung und Unterhaltung.*

# Millennium Dome, UK

1996–1999

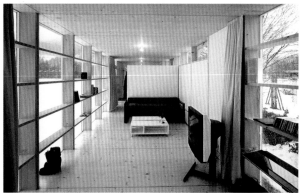

### Ready-to-use housing
*Ein bezugsfertiges Haus*

**Design:** Johannes Kaufmann

Austrian architect Johannes Kaufmann has developed many modular-based housing projects over the years. His basic concept was to provide ready-to-use dwellings (possibly even ordered by catalogue) that could be delivered in a few weeks and equipped with every comfort necessary. SU-SI is the pinnacle of his efforts, a one-storey prefabricated house raised off the ground on a system of stilts. Accessed via ladder, the SU-SI can be transported on the back of a flatbed and, once delivered, assembled in just five hours. The materials used in the construction include steel and glass for the exterior and wood for the interior. Its style is truly rational, as evidenced throughout the kitchen, bathroom and home furnishings.

*Der österreichische Architekt Johannes Kaufmann hat über mehrere Jahre hinweg verschiedene modulare Wohnsysteme entwickelt: Ihm schwebte ein bezugsfertiges, eventuell nach Katalog bestellbares Haus vor, das bereits wenige Wochen nach Anforderung inklusive jeglichem Komfort lieferbar sein sollte. Das Ergebnis dieser Überlegungen ist SU-SI: ein einstöckiges Fertighaus, das auf einem Lastwagen transportiert werden kann. Am Zielort wird es innerhalb von nur fünf Stunden montiert und auf ein Pfeilersystem aufgeständert. Der Zugang erfolgt über eine Treppe. Für die Verkleidung kommen außen Stahl und Glas sowie im Inneren Holz zum Einsatz. Die Ausstattung besteht aus Küche, Bad und Mobiliar in rationalistischem Design.*

**Countryside unit**
*Ein Loft auf dem Land*

**Design:** Lacaton & Vassal

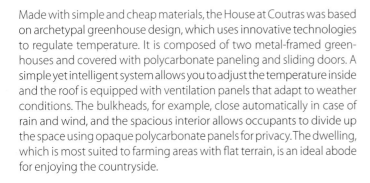

Made with simple and cheap materials, the House at Coutras was based on archetypal greenhouse design, which uses innovative technologies to regulate temperature. It is composed of two metal-framed greenhouses and covered with polycarbonate paneling and sliding doors. A simple yet intelligent system allows you to adjust the temperature inside and the roof is equipped with ventilation panels that adapt to weather conditions. The bulkheads, for example, close automatically in case of rain and wind, and the spacious interior allows occupants to divide up the space using opaque polycarbonate panels for privacy. The dwelling, which is most suited to farming areas with flat terrain, is an ideal abode for enjoying the countryside.

*Dieses Haus in Coutras wurde mit einfachen, preiswerten Materialien realisiert. Es geht auf die typische Gewächshausarchitektur zurück, dessen innovative Technologien der Temperaturregulierung es für sich nutzt. Das Metallgerüst dieser zwei nebeneinanderstehende Häuser ist mit Polycarbonatplatten verkleidet und mit Schiebetüren ausgestattet. Ein einfaches und intelligentes System regelt die Temperatur im Inneren. Auf dem Dach sind Lüftungsplatten installiert, die sich den Wetterverhältnissen anpassen: Bei Regen und Wind schließen sich die Schotten automatisch. Der große, offene Innenbereich ermöglicht verschiedene Möglichkeiten der Raumaufteilung. In Coutras sind die privaten Bereiche mit undurchsichtigen Wänden aus Polycarbonat verkleidet. Diese Art Wohnhaus eignet sich für ländliche Gebiete mit flachem Gelände – ideal für alle, die das Leben im Freien genießen.*

 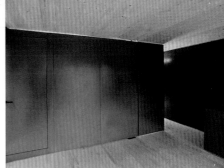

## Garden living
### *Wohnen im Garten*

**Design:** Ivan Kroupa

Ivan Kroupa, creator of Mukarov House, defines his creation as "not a house with a garden, but a garden with a house," since the vegetation that surrounds it seems like an extension of the interior. The wooden structure, with its metal core, is characterized by large windows that allow visual integration of the interior and exterior. Another connection between yard and home is the wooden base of the unit, which extends out to become the terrace. Wood is the characteristic element of the house, lining the walls, ceiling, and floor. The partitions are movable, offering numerous spatial configurations within the dwelling. The overall feel is minimalist but welcoming, and the functionality of Mukarov House makes it suitable for anything from family abode to artist atelier.

*Ivan Kroupa, der Erfinder des Mukarov House, nennt seinen Entwurf nicht „Haus mit Garten", sondern „Garten mit Haus", weil sich der Innenraum gleichsam in die umgebende Vegetation auszudehnen scheint. In die Holzstruktur fügt sich ein Kern aus Metall mit großen Fensterfronten ein, die Innen und Außen zu einer Einheit werden lassen. Die Verbindung von Wohnbereich und Garten ist durch die Basis aus Holz gegeben, die ins Grün hinauswächst und als Terrasse dient. Holz als charakteristisches Material taucht bei der Verkleidung der Wände und der Decke sowie beim Fußbodenbelag wieder auf. Die Trennwände sind beweglich und bieten verschiedene Möglichkeiten der Raumaufteilung. Der großzügige, minimal gestaltete, aber durchaus einladende Innenraum und die Funktionalität machen Mukarov zu einem Haus, das unterschiedlichen Ansprüchen gerecht wird: Bevor es zum Künstleratelier wurde, hatte hier eine Familie gewohnt.*

**Traveling museum**
*Museum auf Reisen*

**Design:** Atelier Van Lieshout

The Good, the Bad, and the Ugly is a travelling structure that was commissioned by the Walker Art Center in Minneapolis to bring art and culture to schools in even the poorest neighborhoods in the state. The name commemorates Sergio Leone's masterpiece Western and was chosen by the designer to mimic real life, where good and evil co-exist. The two modules of the project signify each of these states. The trailer and its extension represent "good", while "evil" is symbolized by the frightening, black wooden shack module. Both spaces contain activities geared toward children, the project's target group. The interior is spartan, clad in recycled wood, but equipped with tables, chairs, a bed, and a stove to provide heat.

*„The Good, the Bad and the Ugly" („Das Gute, das Böse und das Hässliche") ist ein aus mehreren Teilen bestehender fahrbarer Baukörper, der vom Walker Art Center in Minneapolis in Auftrag gegeben wurde, um die Schulen der ärmsten Gegenden des gleichnamigen Bundesstaats mit einem Kunst- und Kulturvermittlungsprogramm zu erreichen. Der Name erinnert an den meisterhaften Western von Sergio Leone und bringt die Absicht der Designer zum Ausdruck, das reale Leben darzustellen, in dem Gut und Böse nebeneinander bestehen. Deshalb gehört außer dem Anhänger und seinem Annex auch noch ein schwarzes Holzhaus zum Projekt: „böse" und isoliert steht es im Wald. Der Anhänger verkörpert das Gute, seine Erweiterung das Hässliche: In diesen Räumen finden während der Fahrt die Angebote für Kinder statt. Die schlicht gehaltenen Innenräume sind mit Recyclingholz verkleidet und mit Tischen, Stühlen, einem Bett und einem Heizofen ausgestattet.*

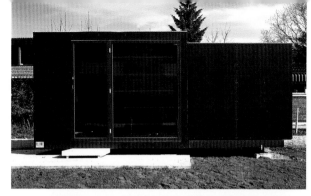

## A home constructed in hours
*Hausbau innerhalb weniger Stunden*

**Design:** Johannes Kaufmann

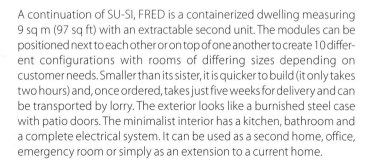

A continuation of SU-SI, FRED is a containerized dwelling measuring 9 sq m (97 sq ft) with an extractable second unit. The modules can be positioned next to each other or on top of one another to create 10 different configurations with rooms of differing sizes depending on customer needs. Smaller than its sister, it is quicker to build (it only takes two hours) and, once ordered, takes just five weeks for delivery and can be transported by lorry. The exterior looks like a burnished steel case with patio doors. The minimalist interior has a kitchen, bathroom and a complete electrical system. It can be used as a second home, office, emergency room or simply as an extension to a current home.

*FRED, die Weiterentwicklung des Fertighauses SU-SI, ist eine Wohnzelle von 3 x 3 m, in der sich eine weitere ausziehbare Einheit gleicher Größe verbirgt. Die Module können miteinander kombiniert, nebeneinander- oder auch übereinandergestellt werden. Insgesamt ergeben sich so – je nach Bedarf des Kunden – zehn verschiedene Haustypen mit unterschiedlich großen Räumen. FRED ist als „kleiner Bruder" von SU-SI noch schneller zu montieren (in nur zwei Stunden), wird innerhalb von fünf Wochen nach Bestellung ausgeliefert und kann auf einem Lastwagen transportiert werden. Von außen erscheint das Modell wie eine Box aus brüniertem Stahl mit einer großen Glastür. Die minimalistische Inneneinrichtung besteht aus einer Küche, einem Bad und Elektroanschlüssen. Das Wohnmodul kann als Zweithaus, Notunterkunft, Büro oder auch als Erweiterung einer vorhandenen Wohnung genutzt werden.*

**From module to house: modular and ecological**
*Vom Modul zum Haus: wandelbar und ökologisch*

**Design:** Michael Jantzen

M-House is a futuristic modular structure that can be adapted to a variety of needs such as a home or a pavilion. It consists of a series of rectangular panels assembled in different ways to create the living unit you desire. The module can then be dismantled, transported and reassembled in another location. Of particular note with this solution is that an entire house can be constructed using the basic panel model along with the windows, doors, roofs and even the structure's interior decor. It is also environmentally friendly: Its creator, California architect Michael Jantzen, is a scholar of low-impact modular buildings that exploit solar and wind energy alternatives.

*Das modular aufgebaute, futuristisch anmutende M-House ist äußerst vielseitig und passt sich den jeweiligen Anforderungen an. Es besteht aus mehreren rechteckigen Wandelementen, die sich auf verschiedene Weisen nach Belieben zu einer Wohneinheit zusammensetzen lassen. Diese kann anschließend abgebaut, transportiert und an einem anderen Ort wieder aufgebaut werden. Das Besondere daran ist, dass die gesamte Konstruktion mit Fenstern, Türen und Überdachung inklusive der Einrichtung aus ein und demselben Grundelement besteht. Das M-House kann zum Wohnen, als Pavillon für Messen oder auch als Büro- und Geschäftsgebäude dienen. Außerdem ist es umweltverträglich: Sein Erfinder, der kalifornische Architekt Michael Jantzen, gehört zu den großen Kennern und Entwicklern einer modularen, umweltschonenden Architektur, die auf Sonnen- und Windenergie setzt.*

# 4

from 2000 to now

---

von 2000 bis heute

## The new millennium brings greater awareness in architecture and design

Concern for the environment has taken on an increasingly important role as designers begin to focus on sustainable timber, photovoltaic cells and water recycling systems. One only has to look at the self-sufficient units of Cannatà & Fernandes or R-House, the vacation home designed by Michael Jantzen. Ecology does not just denote a respect for nature; it mandates that you live in contact with it. There are many projects positioned in the countryside or by the sea, such as Joshua Tree by the Hangar Design Group.

But it is not just ecology that has dominated the recent movement. Another central theme is emergency response in which lightweight mobile units are easily transported and easy to assemble on site.

Prefabrication is experiencing a profound transition right now. The market demands that design and construction times be reduced, not only in residential projects but also in schools, shops and hotels. Examples such as PUMA City by LOT-EK, the FREITAG Shop by Spillmann Echsle in Zurich or houses by Jennifer Siegal were all delivered preassembled on the back of trucks.

Advances in vehicle design have been significant as well, offering all of the creature comforts, technology and appliances we have come to expect from our stationary homes. The Volkner Mobil offers high-tech luxury, for example, while the Bookbus, a library on wheels, offers a unique learning experience.

## Das neue Jahrtausend – ein gewandeltes Bewusstsein in Architektur und Design

*Das Interesse an den Themen Umweltschutz und Nachhaltigkeit wächst. Die Architekten beginnen, Naturhölzern und Bioklebern den Vorzug zu geben, und setzen immer häufiger Fotovoltaikanlagen und Wasseraufbereitungssysteme ein. Beispiele hierfür sind die energetisch autarken Wohneinheiten von Cannatà & Fernandes und das erstaunliche Feriendomizil R-House von Michael Jantzen. Ökologie bedeutet nicht nur, die Natur zu respektieren, sondern auch, in Kontakt mit ihr zu leben. Kleine Wohnhäuser werden entworfen, die am Strand oder mitten im Grünen platzierbar sind, wie das Modell Joshua Tree von der Hangar Design Group. Neben dem Umweltbewusstsein sind Notunterkünfte ein weiteres zentrales Thema: Die Antwort liefern kleine, leichte und mobile Wohneinheiten, die einfach zu transportieren und rasch am gewünschten Standort aufzubauen sind.*

*Der Fertigbau erfährt derzeit international große Aufmerksamkeit. Die Gesellschaft verlangt nach immer kürzeren Planungs- und Bauzeiten: Nicht nur Wohnungen, auch Geschäfte, Schulen und Hotels müssen diesen Anforderungen genügen. So entstanden der Bau PUMA City vom Studio LOT-EK, der FREITAG Shop Zürich von Spillmann Echsle oder die fertig montierten, per Lkw lieferbaren Häuser von Jennifer Siegal.*

*Die Wohnmobile ähneln unterdessen mehr und mehr regelrechten fahrbaren Gebäuden. Sie bieten Komfort und viele Extras wie das luxuriöse Volkner Mobil oder der fast märchenhafte Bookbus, eine Bibliothek auf Rädern, die zu einer kulturellen Reise einlädt.*

## Cocooning oneself to defend nature
*Umgeben von einem Kokon, um die Natur zu verteidigen*

**Design:** Santiago Cirugeda

In 2001, the municipality of Seville made the decision to remove some trees in the historic Alameda Square to make way for an underground car park. Independently and spontaneously, citizens built shelters to demonstrate their disappointment, creating an airborne village of protesters called "Villa Ardilla". Santiago Cirugeda's module was equipped with a pantry for supplies and a ventilation system to keep people cool in the summer heat – a new take on the classic tree house, this time with a modern, aerodynamic form. Quick and easy to install, the new design is also a throwback to medieval defensive ramparts. But this incarnation, which allows the module to be anchored to the tree without damaging it, carries a very clear message: To live harmoniously with nature, we must also be able to defend it.

*Als die Stadt Sevilla 2001 die Abholzung von Bäumen auf der historischen Plaza Alameda beschloss, um eine Tiefgarage zu bauen, äußerte sich Protest in Form eines „Villa Ardilla" (dt. „Eichhörnchendorf") genannten Luftdorfes: Mehrere Bürger bauten sich unabhängig und spontan Hütten, um ihre Empörung zum Ausdruck zu bringen. Santiago Cirugeda stattete sein Häuschen mit einer Vorratskammer und einem Ventilator gegen die Sommerhitze aus. Das altbekannte Baumhaus überlässt so neuen, aerodynamischen, einfach und schnell zu montierenden Bauformen seinen Platz: ein Rückgriff auf mittelalterliche Belagerungsmethoden, der über den beabsichtigten Protest hinaus auch für eine Art Höhencamping Verwendung finden könnte – und eine originelle Provokation, die es ermöglicht, sich in einem Baum zu verankern, ohne ihn zu verletzen. Doch die Casa Insecta transportiert noch eine weitere, eindeutige Botschaft: Wer in Verbindung mit der Natur leben will, muss auch in der Lage sein, sie zu schützen.*

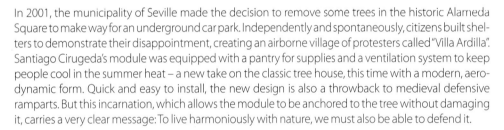

**120**

### Like an Impressionist painting: the Maison flottante
*Wie in einem impressionistischen Gemälde: die Maison flottante*

**Design:** Ronan and Erwan Bouroullec

Maison flottante is a charming, temporary studio residence for the artist guests of CNEAI (a national contemporary art center) in Chatou, France. Constructed on a 20-m (65-ft) platform, the lightweight aluminum core is lined with wood and drifts elegantly along the Seine. The atmosphere of the module is in perfect harmony with nature, and lends itself wonderfully to either a living or workspace. Created by the *enfants terribles* of French design, the Bouroullec brothers, it is a pragmatic response to the project's allocated budget. The result is a simple design in which nothing detracts from the poetic purity of the outcome. The interior's elegant and minimalist decor is flooded with light from two large windows, a nod to Chatou's magical past as the Impressionists' Island.

*Die Maison flottante ist ein bezauberndes Wohnatelier für temporäre Aufenthalte von Gastkünstlern des Centre National de l'estampe et de l'art imprimé in Chatou, Frankreich. Auf einer etwa 20 m langen schwimmenden Plattform bewegt es sich sanft über die Seine. Eine leichte, mit Holz ausgekleidete Aluminiumstruktur definiert den Wohnraum, in dem es sich in perfekter Harmonie mit Umgebung und Natur arbeiten lässt. Der Entwurf der Brüder Bouroullec, zweier „enfants terribles" des französischen Designs, versteht sich als Antwort auf das geringe Budget, das für das Projekt zur Verfügung stand, ohne dass die schlichte Struktur dem poetischen Gesamteindruck und einer konsequenten Gestaltung jedoch schaden würde. Die elegante, moderne Einrichtung erstrahlt im Licht, das durch die großen Fensterfronten einfällt und an die magische Vergangenheit Chatous – der einstigen „Insel der Impressionisten" – erinnert.*

Maison flottante, France                    2002–2006

**Container accommodation: mobile & functional**
*Wohnen im Container: mobil & funktional*

**Design:** LOT-EK (Ada Tolla, Giuseppe Lignano)

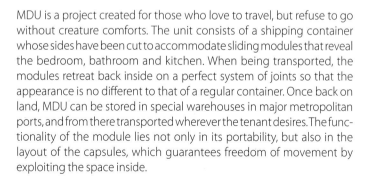

MDU is a project created for those who love to travel, but refuse to go without creature comforts. The unit consists of a shipping container whose sides have been cut to accommodate sliding modules that reveal the bedroom, bathroom and kitchen. When being transported, the modules retreat back inside on a perfect system of joints so that the appearance is no different to that of a regular container. Once back on land, MDU can be stored in special warehouses in major metropolitan ports, and from there transported wherever the tenant desires. The functionality of the module lies not only in its portability, but also in the layout of the capsules, which guarantees freedom of movement by exploiting the space inside.

*MDU ist ein Entwurf für alle, die gern reisen, ohne dabei auf Annehmlichkeiten verzichten zu wollen. Es besteht aus einem Container mit ausziehbaren „Schubladen" an den Seiten, die als Wohn- oder Arbeitsplatzeinheiten dienen: Über einen Rollmechanismus treten ganze Module aus dem Container hervor, die etwa das Bett, das Bad oder die Küche beinhalten. Während der Reise ziehen sich die Einheiten wie bei einem perfekten Schubladensystem ins Innere zurück, der Container nimmt wieder seine normalen Dimensionen an und kann überallhin verschifft werden. Am Zielhafen wird er in einer Lagerhalle deponiert und von hier aus an den gewünschten Standort befördert. Praktisch an dem Konzept MDU ist nicht nur die Transportfähigkeit, sondern auch das zweckmäßig eingerichtete Innere, das unter bestmöglicher Ausnutzung des vorhandenen Raumes Bewegungsfreiheit gewährleistet.*

**Ready to go in just a few weeks**
*Innerhalb weniger Wochen einsatzfähig*

Design: Tim Pyne

A cross between a caravan and a house, M-House arrives at your chosen destination in two flat-packed boxes and is assembled on site. Each block is equipped with wheels, which makes transportation of the unit both easy and efficient, and will make any journey from the city to the countryside or seashore a fun experience. The front of the structure rests on a wooden platform, which also acts as a terrace. The wood-paneled interior of M-House resembles a standard abode with kitchen, bedroom and fully-equipped bathroom, but it can also be used as an office. The atmosphere inside invites you to hang pictures and add furniture, or you can add a personal touch by customising the layout of the partitions.

*M-House, eine Kombination aus Wohnwagen und Haus, erreicht seinen Zielort in zwei Teilen, die erst vor Ort miteinander verbunden werden. Jedes Teil hat zwei Räder, genau wie ein Wohnwagen – entsprechend einfach und schnell geht der Transport, und die Fahrt von der Stadt aufs Land oder ans Meer ist kurzweilig. Am Wunschort angekommen, wird das Vorderteil auf eine hölzerne Plattform aufgesetzt, die gleichzeitig als Terrasse dient. Innen sieht das M-House wie ein gewöhnliches Haus aus, kann jedoch auch als Büro genutzt werden. Es stehen eine Küche, ein Schlafzimmer sowie ein Bad mit Dusche und Wanne zur Verfügung. Die Wandverkleidung aus Holz schafft eine einladende Atmosphäre und ermöglicht das Anbringen von Bildern und Möbeln. Der Besitzer kann außerdem die Trennwände nach Belieben verschieben, um den Raum individuell zu gestalten.*

**The self-sufficient home**
*Das Selbstversorgerhaus*

**Design:** Cannatà & Fernandes

As its name suggests, this unit is energy self-sufficient. On the roof is a photovoltaic panel that provides enough power to charge batteries that can run the house for three days. It also features a water recycling system. Due to its compact size (9 x 3 x 3m), Capa can be easily transported and adapted to any landscape, integrating seamlessly with its surroundings. Its aesthetic appearance is defined by a minimalist form, but the interior is equipped with all the necessary creature comforts. The unit can also take on a variety of functions, morphing from vacation cabin to emergency room for example, or it can be connected to other modules to create a more permanent structure.

*Wie sein Name schon sagt, versorgt sich dieses Wohnmodul selbst mit Energie. Das Dach ruht auf einer Metallstruktur und ist mit einer Fotovoltaikanlage ausgestattet, die ausreichend Strom für drei Tage produziert; außerdem ist ein System zur Wasseraufbereitung vorhanden. Das Modul lässt sich dank seiner geringen Größe von nur 9 x 3 x 3 m bequem per Lastwagen transportieren und passt sich in jede Umgebung ein. Ein modernes Design bestimmt das äußere Erscheinungsbild, die Einrichtung ist ausgesprochen komfortabel. Es kann zum Beispiel als Ferienwohnung oder als Notunterkunft dienen, aber auch mit weiteren Modulen zu einem regelrechten Hotel erweitert werden.*

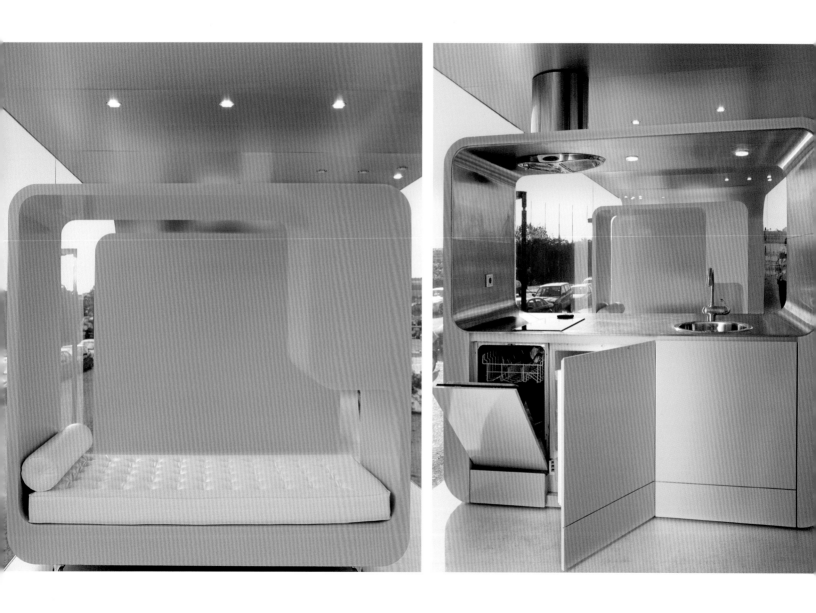

### Ecology on an industrial scale
*Ökologie auf Industrieniveau*

**Design:** Cannatà & Fernandes

As a twin to the Capa mobile unit, the DST module was designed to accommodate a wider range of functions, from a meeting place or small bar to an observatory or firefighters' control room. The unit is ideally suited to them all and can be placed in any terrain, but it is most effective in areas where basic infrastructure is not tenable, such as national parks. The project itself represents the symbiosis of industrial production, energy conservation and ecological integration concepts. DST is equipped with photovoltaic panels and other features that provide the module with sufficient electricity and water, and the designers paid particular attention to ecologically-friendly construction methods and materials. As a result, the structure is made entirely of wood so that it can blend in with its environment.

*Als Zwillingsbruder der Wohneinheit Capa ist das Modul DST für eine ganze Reihe von Funktionen vorgesehen. Es eignet sich beispielsweise perfekt als kleine Bar oder Treffpunkt, aber auch als Messestand, Naturwarte oder Feuerwachkabine. Das Modul kann auf jeglichem Gelände aufgestellt werden und ist insbesondere auch für Orte wie Naturparks gedacht, an denen keine Infrastruktur eingerichtet werden kann. Die Planer sahen eine ideale Verbindung aus industrieller Herstellung, Umweltverträglichkeits- und Energiesparprinzipien vor: So verfügt das Haus über eine Fotovoltaikanlage und versorgt sich hinsichtlich Strom und Warmwasserbereitung selbst. Auch betreffs der Bauweise setzt der Entwurf auf Nachhaltigkeit und eine präzise Wahl der Materialien; das Modul besteht komplett aus Holz und erscheint somit am entsprechenden Aufstellungsort als Teil der umgebenden Landschaft.*

**A simple, and ecological lifestyle**

*Für einen einfachen, umweltfreundlichen Lebensstil*

**Design:** Michelle Kaufmann

Low environmental impact is the catchword for this project. Built using the most innovative methods available, Glidehouse® is made exclusively from factory-made prefab parts with an estimated construction time of around a year. The materials used are all environmentally friendly. The wood is Forest Stewardship Certified (FSC), the eco-resin is generated from 30 per cent recycled content, and the internal flooring is made of bamboo with the exception of the bathroom, which is tiled with recycled glass. A great deal of attention was focused on the HVAC system. The mechanical system filters and recycles outside air, creating hot air in winter and cool air in summer. Composed of modules, it can be replicated if required. Glidehouse® is characterized by its pure and elegant form.

*Das Glidehouse® steht für umweltfreundliches Wohnen. Es wurde mithilfe neuester Baumethoden und ausschließlich aus Fertigbauteilen errichtet, die in etwa einem Jahr in der Fabrik hergestellt werden. Dabei kommen ausschließlich ökologische Materialien zum Einsatz: Das Holz ist vom Forest Stewardship Council zertifiziert, das Bioharz wird zu 30 % aus Recyclingkomponenten gewonnen, der Fußbodenbelag in den Innenräumen besteht aus Bambus, und in den Bädern sind Fliesen aus Recyclingglas verlegt. Besondere Sorgfalt wurde auch auf die Klimatisierung der Räume gelegt – ein mechanisches System filtert die Außenluft, bereitet sie auf und erzeugt im Winter warme, im Sommer kühle Luft. Das Haus mit seinen klaren, eleganten Formen besteht aus Modulen, kann also identisch kopiert werden.*

## The spirituality of contemporary life
### *Die Spiritualität zeitgenössischen Lebens*

**Design:** Ecosistema urbano

This prefabricated structure is raised off the ground on steel poles, can adapt to just about any slope and is minimally invasive with regard to the environment. Living in it, one has the feeling of being completely immersed in nature, as if the house were an integral part of the landscape. The dwelling is designed to face south and with its large front windows and vertical slots filtering the light it ensures maximum exposure to the sun. The nucleus of the building is steel, but the interior and exterior are clad in wood, reminiscent of old mountain cottages. The result is simple and pure – even somewhat monastic. Despite acknowledging the past, its rational lines make it truly contemporary.

*Dieses Fertighaus passt sich jedem Gefälle an: Der Baukörper ist unter Berücksichtigung von Gelände und Baumbestand auf unterschiedlich hohe Stahlpfeiler aufgeständert. Seine Bewohner fühlen sich vollkommen in die Natur integriert, so als wäre das Haus ein Bestandteil der Landschaft. Die großen Fensterfronten sind nach Süden ausgerichtet, um möglichst viel Sonnenlicht zu erhalten. Vertikale Einschnitte lassen das Licht seitlich einfallen. Die Tragkonstruktion aus Stahl ist sowohl außen als auch innen mit Holz verkleidet, was an die traditionelle Berghütte erinnert. Die rationalistische Linienführung wiederum hebt das Haus deutlich von den Formen der Vergangenheit ab und macht es zu einem betont zeitgenössisch gestalteten Bauwerk. Das Ergebnis ist eine schlichte, konsequent durchgestaltete Wohneinheit. Sie ähnelt in gewisser Weise einem Kloster, zu dessen Glaubensbekenntnis eine friedliche Natur gehört.*

# House of Steel and Wood, Spain

2003–2005

**Panoramic multi-use loft**
*Das multifunktionale Panoramahaus*

**Design:** Werner Aisslinger

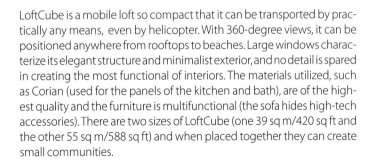

LoftCube is a mobile loft so compact that it can be transported by practically any means, even by helicopter. With 360-degree views, it can be positioned anywhere from rooftops to beaches. Large windows characterize its elegant structure and minimalist exterior, and no detail is spared in creating the most functional of interiors. The materials utilized, such as Corian (used for the panels of the kitchen and bath), are of the highest quality and the furniture is multifunctional (the sofa hides high-tech accessories). There are two sizes of LoftCube (one 39 sq m/420 sq ft and the other 55 sq m/588 sq ft) and when placed together they can create small communities.

*Der LoftCube ist ein mobiles Loft mit offenem Charakter und kann bequem mit unterschiedlichen Verkehrsmitteln transportiert werden (auch im Hubschrauber). Er ist nicht nur für normales Gelände geeignet, sondern kann beispielsweise auch auf einem Flachdach oder am Strand aufgestellt werden. Sein moderner, minimalistischer Stil mit eleganten Pilotis und großen Fenstern setzt sich auch innen fort: Strenge und formale Konsequenz prägen den funktionalen Raum, in dem selbst kleinste Details durchdacht sind. Die eingesetzten Materialien, darunter Corian für Verkleidungen in Küche und Bad, sind sehr hochwertig, und jeder Einrichtungsgegenstand erfüllt mehrere Funktionen (im Sofa verbergen sich zum Beispiel Hightechaccessoires). Die LoftCube-Wohneinheiten sind in den zwei Standardgrößen 39 und 55 m$^2$ erhältlich, können aber auch zu richtigen Dörfern miteinander verbunden werden.*

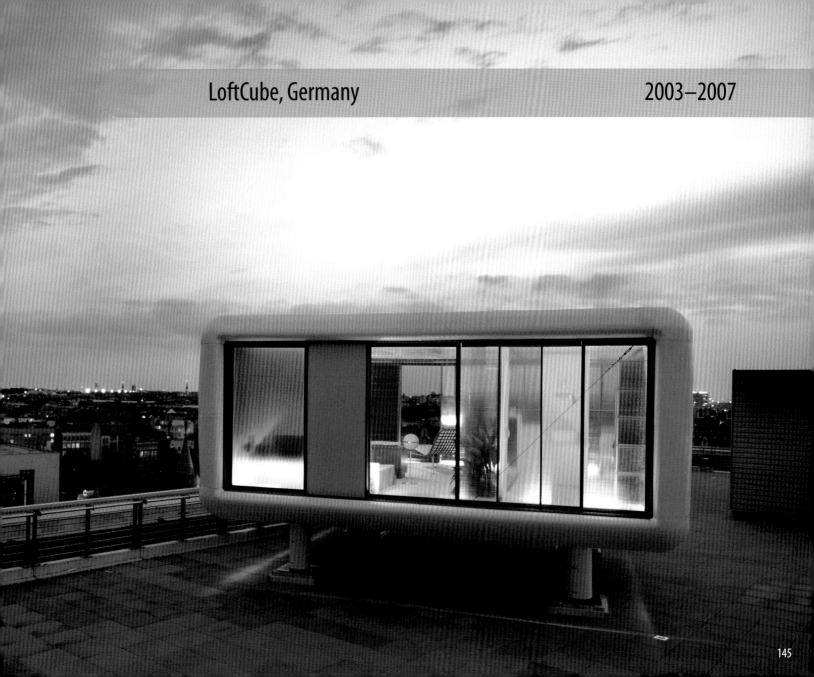

## Adobe sacks for emergency housing
### *Lehmsäcke für Notunterkünfte*

**Design:** Nader Khalili

Superadobe homes, which look more like a gnome's abode than emergency housing, use a special construction technique conceived by architect Nader Khalili and his Cal-Earth non-profit organization. Based on the ancient building material adobe (a mixture of sand, clay, and straw used by the indigenous peoples of North, Central and South America), Khalili developed superadobe, which can be used to construct entire villages. Each structure of up to 40 m (131 ft) in diameter is created using polypropylene bags filled with superadobe. The bags are stacked in a circular pattern, creating a waterproof dome, with barbed wire placed between each layer to ensure the dwelling can withstand hurricanes. Superadobe is an ideal material because it is both cheap and fire-retardant. Each unit is designed to be equipped with solar panels.

*Sie sehen aus wie Zwergenhäuser, sind aber Notunterkünfte. Ihr Erfinder, Nader Khalili, hat in Zusammenarbeit mit der kalifornischen Non-Profit-Organisation Cal Earth eine spezielle Bautechnik entwickelt. Ausgehend von dem alten Werkstoff Adobe, eine von den Völkern Mittelamerikas verwendete Mischung aus Stroh und Lehm, erfand er Superadobe, mit dem man ganze Dörfer errichten kann. Die Baukörper bestehen aus Polypropylensäcken mit einem Durchmesser von etwa 40 cm, die mit Sand oder Lehm gefüllt werden. Die Säcke werden im Kreis aufeinandergestapelt und bilden so eine Kuppelform; jeweils zwischen zwei Schichten befindet sich eine Lage Stacheldraht. Superadobe stellt ein optimales Baumaterial dar: Es ist preiswert und wärmeisolierend. Dank ihrer Halbkugelform halten die Wohnhäuser auch Regen und Wirbelstürme aus. Jede Wohneinheit kann außerdem mit Solarzellen versehen werden.*

**Technology, ecology and luxury for the mobile house**
*Technologie, Ökologie und Luxus für das tragbare Haus*

**Design:** OMD (Jennifer Siegal)

OMD ShowHouse is a portable house (transported on trucks) that features new concepts of flexibility and use of compact spaces. Designed to be built in phases, it is entirely prefabricated and can be transported and positioned anywhere you desire, from urban centers to the countryside. The first one is in Venice, California, and is used by its designer, Jennifer Siegal, as a model home for prospective buyers. The interior, which offers nearly 70 sq m (753 sq ft) of usable space, is precise and elegant, combining technology, ecology and well-known brands for everything from the sound system to the air-conditioning. Panels and flooring are made from bamboo and coconut. The rational design of the exterior is clad with metal and translucent polycarbonate siding.

*Das OMD ShowHouse ist tragbar, äußerst flexibel und kompakt und kann per Lastwagen transportiert werden. Als Fertighaus wurde es für die Serienproduktion entwickelt, wird noch an der Produktionsstätte vollständig montiert, anschließend an den Wunschort in der Stadt oder auf dem Land befördert und aufgestellt. Das erste Modell befindet sich im kalifornischen Venice, wo es seiner Schöpferin Jennifer Siegal als Musterhaus dient. Die Innenräume mit insgesamt fast 70 m² Wohnfläche wurden mit großer Sorgfalt und Eleganz eingerichtet. Sie vereinen Technologie und Ökologie mit luxuriösen Details namhafter Marken und verfügen außerdem über ein raffiniertes Audiosystem sowie eine Klimaanlage. Abdeckungen und Fußbodenbeläge bestehen aus Bambus und Kokos. Die zweckmäßig gestalteten Fassaden sind mit Metall und transparenten Polykarbonatplatten verkleidet.*

**A shipping container skyscraper**
*Ein Wolkenkratzer aus Containern*

**Design:** Spillmann Echsle (Harald Echsle)

In 2008, the retail brand FREITAG won the first annual Swiss Marketing + Architecture Award for Best Store. Designed by architecture firm Spillmann Echsle, the F-Shop was based on the principle that FREITAG implemented for its bags, which are composed of recycled truck tarpaulin and seat belts and originally took inspiration from the transportation industry. To create the structure, seventeen recycled shipping containers were transported by train from Hamburg to Zurich and placed on top of each other, nine high and four wide. Some of the containers' steel walls have been removed to create huge windows while white cardboard boxes display FREITAG's stylish products inside.

*Der F-Shop, ein vom Architekturbüro Spillmann Echsle in Zürich für die Marke FREITAG entworfenes Geschäft, ist Preisträger des schweizerischen „Award für Marketing + Architektur" in der Kategorie „Warenhäuser, Läden, Kundencenter und Flagship Stores". Wie die FREITAG-Taschen (sie bestehen aus Lkw-Planen und Sicherheitsgurten) orientiert sich auch der F-Shop an der Welt des Transports. Siebzehn alte Container wurden dafür mit der Bahn von Hamburg nach Zürich transportiert und zu einem neunstöckigen Turm aufeinandergestapelt, der sich horizontal in vier Bereiche weiterentwickelt. Einige Stahlwände hat man aufgeschnitten, um sie durch riesige Fensterflächen zu ersetzen. Im Geschäft werden die Taschen auf Sockeln und in Schubladen aus weißem Karton nach einem strengen, aber ästhetisch äußerst wirksamen Prinzip präsentiert.*

**154**

## Luxury vacations in an RV with garage
### *Luxusurlaub im Wohnmobil mit Autobox*

**Design:** Volkner Mobil

With its debut at the Dusseldorf International Caravan Fair in 2006, the Volkner Mobil Performance is a camper so large it can accommodate a small car inside its body. Built on a Mercedes bus chassis, this luxury hotel suite on wheels has wowed the public since its launch. It features a dining room, kitchen, bathroom and bedroom all fitted with floor heating and a Dolby Surround sound system. The interior draws on luxury yacht design with wooden paneling and furnishings, leather couches, carpeting and panoramic windows. It is a vehicle very much geared for an upscale market and certainly restricted to just a handful of enthusiasts.

*Man stelle sich ein Wohnmobil mit so großen Ausmaßen vor, dass in seinem Inneren sogar ein Auto auf einer ausziehbaren Plattform Platz findet: Das Volkner Mobil Performance, ein regelrechtes Haus auf Rädern, löste bei den Besuchern der internationalen Wohnmobil- und Caravanmesse 2006 in Düsseldorf Staunen und Bewunderung aus – und nicht nur seiner Größe wegen. Konstruiert wie ein eleganter Mercedes-Bus, verfügt das Fahrzeug über ein Esszimmer, eine Küche, ein Bad und ein Schlafzimmer. Seine Ausstattung ist mit Fußbodenheizung und Dolby-Surround-System so raffiniert und komfortabel, wie man es von einer Hotelsuite erwarten würde. Die Ledersofas, die holzverkleideten Wände und Möbel, die Teppichböden und Panoramafenster unter der Decke erinnern an den Einrichtungsstil einer Yacht: ein sicherlich wenigen Käufern vorbehaltenes Wohnmobil aus dem Luxussegment.*

**Culture travels by bus**
*Kultur auf Reisen*

Design: Muungano (Peter Thuvander, Martin Hedenström)

Muungano, a Swedish design studio whose name means *solidarity* in Swahili, has developed a traveling library concept for the Arctic Circle municipality of Kiruna. The bus brings a wealth of information to the 32 villages in the province, which is otherwise pretty isolated from standard print media. The exterior by Fredic Forsberg is youthful and evokes a *street style* while the comfortable interior optimizes space and offers a diverse range of activities. In addition to the books on the shelves, the Bookbus has a small movie theater, computers with Internet, CD and video players, and brightly colored sofas. Large windows let in plenty of daylight or allow you to gaze out at the spectacular beauty of the Northern Lights, all while immersing yourself in a good book. Bookbus has won multiple awards, including the Library Bus of the year in 2008.

*Das schwedische Designstudio Muungano („Solidarität" auf Swahili) hat eine Reisebibliothek für die nördlich des Polarkreises gelegene Stadt Kiruna entworfen: Ein Bus versorgt 32 Dörfer der Provinz, die von den Verlagsvertretungen abgeschnitten sind, mit Informationen. Seine grafische Außengestaltung stammt von Fredrik Forsberg, erinnert an den „street style" und fordert Jugendliche zum Zusammenhalt auf. Die komfortable Inneneinrichtung macht sich jeden Winkel zunutze und eröffnet die Möglichkeit zu verschiedenen Aktivitäten: Bookbus hat außer Regalen und Büchern auch ein kleines Kino, Computer mit Internet, Video, CD-Player und farbige Sofas zu bieten. Große Fenster gestatten die optimale Ausnutzung des spärlichen Tageslichts, und bei der Lektüre eines guten Buches kann man das faszinierende Schauspiel des Nordlichts genießen. Muungano hat mehrere Preise erhalten, darunter den „Library Bus of the Year 2008".*

Bookbus, Sweden                                    2006–2008

## Like living in a tree house
*Wohnen wie in einem Baumhaus*

**Design:** olgga architectes

Flake House is a novel, transportable compact mobile house project that can be placed anywhere. More than a dwelling, it was conceived as a shelter... a poetic refuge from the world: it seems to invite a sense of isolation, while seamlessly being a part of nature. It is constructed entirely of wood, in two irregular-shaped modules, the ends of which are open to the elements. Additionally, there is a delightful contrast between the minimalist interior which offers only horizontal apertures on the walls, and the log-covered façade of the exterior.

*Das Flake House ist ein interessanter Entwurf für ein Kompakthaus, das mit einem gewöhnlichen Sattelzug transportiert und an jedem beliebigen Ort aufgestellt werden kann. Weniger als Wohn- denn als poetischer Zufluchtsort konzipiert, lädt es zu Abgeschiedenheit und gleichzeitig zum Dialog mit der Welt ein. Seine zwei Module aus Holz sind unregelmäßig geformt, und die Enden jedes Blocks öffnen sich nach außen. Sehr schön ist der Kontrast zwischen dem minimalistischen Inneren mit seinen schlichten horizontalen Wandöffnungen und der mit Baumstämmen verkleideten Fassade. Das Flake House verfügt mit Küchenbereich und Bad über Basiskomfort.*

## Simple design, green materials
### *Einfache Formen und umweltfreundliche Materialien*

**Design:** Atelier RVL architectes (Jean-Charles Liddell)

MagicKub is an answer to the needs of many a young family: an informal abode, environmentally friendly, and designed to fit a tight budget. It is a large yet simple square-shaped unit with a prefabricated structure and a wooden frame. The materials are all natural (wood and glass), and great attention has been paid to thermal insulation and reducing energy consumption. The unit is easy to assemble and takes just two days to set up. The simplicity of the construction creates an easy-going feel inside the dwelling where spacious interiors offer a bright and youthful ambience. The first floor has high ceilings and houses the dining room and kitchen where a large sliding door opens to the outside. A steel and wood staircase then takes you to the second floor bedrooms and amenities.

*Dieses Wohnhaus wurde auf die Bedürfnisse junger Familien zugeschnitten. Es kommt mit einem bescheidenen Budget aus, wirkt leger und ist umweltfreundlich gestaltet: ein großer, einheitlicher Fertigbaukörper in Form eines Quaders mit einer Tragkonstruktion aus Holz. Die Module sind einfach und schnell innerhalb von nur zwei Tagen zu montieren, wobei ausschließlich natürliche Materialien wie Holz und Glas verwendet werden. Besondere Aufmerksamkeit galt der Wärmeisolierung und einem sparsamen Umgang mit Energie. Die einfache Konstruktion spiegelt sich auch im Inneren wider, die großzügig geschnittenen Zimmer wirken hell und freundlich. Im Erdgeschoss mit doppelter Raumhöhe liegen das Esszimmer und die Küche, eine gläserne Schiebetür öffnet sich in den Außenraum. Eine Treppe aus Stahl und Holz führt ins Obergeschoss zu den Schlaf- und Badezimmern.*

MagicKub, "b(R)ouillon architectural", France        2006–2007

## An ecological prefab duplex
*Ein zweistöckiges Fertighaus auf ökologischer Basis*

Design:   OMD (Jennifer Siegal)

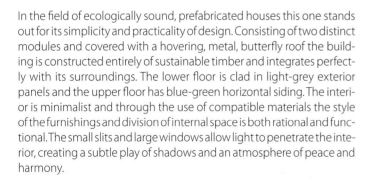

In the field of ecologically sound, prefabricated houses this one stands out for its simplicity and practicality of design. Consisting of two distinct modules and covered with a hovering, metal, butterfly roof the building is constructed entirely of sustainable timber and integrates perfectly with its surroundings. The lower floor is clad in light-grey exterior panels and the upper floor has blue-green horizontal siding. The interior is minimalist and through the use of compatible materials the style of the furnishings and division of internal space is both rational and functional. The small slits and large windows allow light to penetrate the interior, creating a subtle play of shadows and an atmosphere of peace and harmony.

*Dieses Wohnhaus unterscheidet sich von anderen ökologischen Fertigbauhäusern durch seine einfache, zweckmäßige Bauweise: Es umfasst zwei deutlich voneinander abgesetzte, übereinandergestellte Elemente und ein Dach aus Metall. Beide Teile bestehen aus Bioholz, das Erdgeschoss trägt einen glatten, grauen Verputz, und das Obergeschoss ist mit weißem Holz verkleidet. Die Innenraumaufteilung ist zweckvoll und rational, die Ausstattung beweist eine Vorliebe für minimalistisches Design und eine sorgfältige Zusammenstellung der Materialien. Kleine, schlitzförmige Fensteröffnungen lassen im Wechsel mit großen Fenstern das Tageslicht herein, das im Inneren subtile Schattenspiele hervorruft – insgesamt ein dynamisches, perfekt in die Landschaft integriertes Wohnhaus mit einer ruhigen, harmonischen Ausstrahlung.*

**A futuristic pavilion for temporary exhibitions**
*Ein futuristischer Ausstellungspavillon*

**Design:** Architecture and Vision (Arturo Vittori, Andreas Vogler)

Mercury House One is an inhabitable mobile unit, commissioned by Gualtiero Vanelli and manufactured by GVM (Carrara). Conceived as a travelling reception and exhibition space, it is raised from the floor and accessible via a ramp, making it reminiscent of a spaceship. The fiberglass unibody is coated by a thin layer of white marble that creates a remarkable mosaic effect that is backlit at night. The inner surface provides 40 m² (430 square feet) that can be adapted for any display type; and the latest technology in lighting, sound and communications ensure maximum functionality and comfort. The mobile unit is energy autonomous with photovoltaic cells inserted in the roof.

*Das mobile Wohnmodul Mercury House One wurde von dem Italiener Gualtiero Vanelli als reisender Repräsentations- und Empfangspavillon in Auftrag gegeben und von GVM (Carrara) hergestellt . Die äußere Gestalt dieses scheinbar über dem Boden schwebenden, über eine Rampe begehbaren Repräsentations- und Empfangspavillons erinnert an eine Raumkapsel. Die dünne, weiße Marmorbeschichtung seiner selbsttragenden Karosserie aus Fiberglas bildet ein wirkungsvolles Mosaik. Nachts wird das Fahrzeug mittels einer speziellen Durchlichttechnik illuminiert. Der 40 m² große Raum kann je nach Nutzungsart (Events, Vorträge, Ausstellungen, Wohnraum) unterschiedlich eingerichtet werden. Das Modul ist energetisch autark: in den oberen Teil des Daches sind Fotovoltaikzellen eingelassen. Die neuesten Technologien im Bereich der Illumination, des Sounds und der Kommunikation garantieren maximale Funktionalität und höchsten Komfort.*

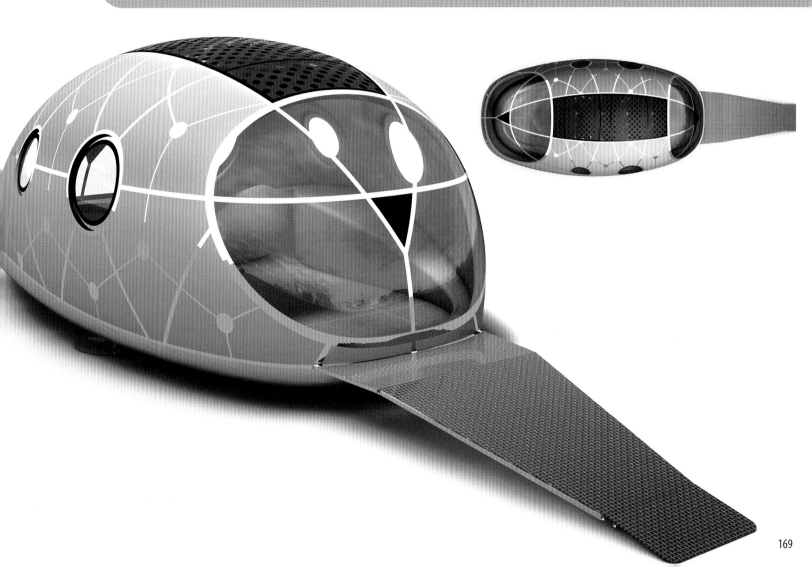

## Mercury House One, Italy      2007–2009

**The little house you can place in the garden**
*Ein kleines Haus, das auch im Garten aufgestellt werden kann*

**Design:** Jonas Wagell

Since January 1st, 2008, every Swedish landowner has had the legal option of building a 15-sq-m (161-sq-ft) house on his or her land without planning permission. Mini House is a prefabricated unit that represents a departure from the typical Northern European cottage and it all began as part of architect and designer Jonas Wagell's thesis. The classic cottages are often similar to the great architectural manors, just smaller, whereas Mini House is a modern design intended for easy assembly and transport. The walls and windows provide good thermal insulation and the pergola-covered terrace provides a charming open-air space. The house can be equipped with solar panels, and the floor plan can be enlarged by adding prefabricated modules such as a kitchen or bathroom.

*Seit dem 1. Januar 2008 darf jeder Schwede, der ein Stück Land besitzt, dieses ohne besondere Genehmigung mit einem Haus von 15 m² Grundfläche bebauen. So konnte der Architekt und Designer Jonas Wagell sein Projekt realisieren. Das Mini House stellt ein Fertighaus dar, das sich stark von der herkömmlichen, typisch nordeuropäischen Bauform der Landhäuser unterscheidet. Während Letztere meist wie Miniaturvillen aussehen, da sie den architektonischen Grundregeln gewöhnlicher großer Wohnhäuser folgen, ist das Mini House modern gestaltet und für den einfachen Transport und Aufbau konzipiert. Die Wände und Einfassungen gewährleisten eine gute Wärmedämmung; eine Pergola umrahmt die Terrasse und sorgt für einen angenehmen Aufenthalt im Freien. Das Haus kann mit Solarzellen ausgerüstet und seine Grundfläche mittels vorgefertigter Module beispielsweise um Bad und Küche erweitert werden.*

## A mobile shop built to follow a regatta
*Ein mobiles Geschäft als Abschluss einer Regatta*

**Design:** LOT-EK (Ada Tolla, Giuseppe Lignano, Keisuke Nibe, Koki Hashimoto)

In 2007, Puma commissioned New York studio LOT-EK to create a new commercial space that could travel the world. The structure would follow the Volvo Ocean Regatta the following year aboard a container ship called the Monster. PUMA City was born. An imposing structure constructed out of 24 entirely interchangeable containers stacked on top of each other, the 12-m-wide (40-ft) store is spread over three levels, two of which are reserved for the sale of the brand's products and the third is a bar with terrace designed for events and concerts. Puma's logo is displayed in large letters on the exterior of the structure. This experimental building represents the first truly mobile building of this scale to be built using shipping containers.

*Im Jahr 2007 beauftragte die Firma Puma das New Yorker Büro LOT-EK mit dem Entwurf eines neuen Verkaufsraums, der um die Welt reisen kann – ein Jahr später sollte er der Regatta „Volvo Ocean" auf einem Frachter namens „Monstrum" folgen. So entstand PUMA City, ein beeindruckendes, vollständig zerlegbares Gebäude aus 24 Containern, die horizontal und vertikal an- und aufeinandermontiert sind. Der 12 m breite Raum entwickelt sich über drei Stockwerke: Zwei sind dem Verkauf von Markenartikeln gewidmet, ein dritter ist mit einer Panoramaterrasse ausgestattet und dient als Bar, für Veranstaltungen und Konzerte. Außen prangt ein riesiges Puma-Logo. Dieser Experimentalbau ist das erste mobile Haus seines Ausmaßes, das aus Containern besteht.*

**History and nature respected by design**

*Ein Entwurf zollt Respekt gegenüber Geschichte und Natur*

**Design:** Fantastic Norway

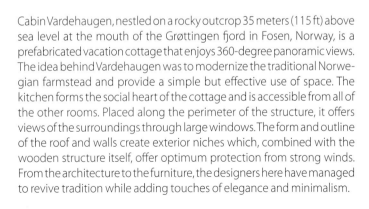

Cabin Vardehaugen, nestled on a rocky outcrop 35 meters (115 ft) above sea level at the mouth of the Grøttingen fjord in Fosen, Norway, is a prefabricated vacation cottage that enjoys 360-degree panoramic views. The idea behind Vardehaugen was to modernize the traditional Norwegian farmstead and provide a simple but effective use of space. The kitchen forms the social heart of the cottage and is accessible from all of the other rooms. Placed along the perimeter of the structure, it offers views of the surroundings through large windows. The form and outline of the roof and walls create exterior niches which, combined with the wooden structure itself, offer optimum protection from strong winds. From the architecture to the furniture, the designers here have managed to revive tradition while adding touches of elegance and minimalism.

*Im Fjord von Grøttingen in Norwegen genießt man von einem 35 m hohen Felshügel aus einen wunderbaren Rundblick. Hier befindet sich Cabin Vardehaugen, ein Fertighaus für Urlaub und Erholung. Seine Planer haben sich von der Architektur der traditionellen norwegischen Gutshäuser mit ihrer einfachen, aber präzisen Raumorganisation inspirieren lassen und sie einer modernen Lesart unterzogen. Die Küche bildet den geselligen Mittelpunkt des Hauses. Alle anderen um sie herum angeordneten Räume öffnen sich mit großen Fensterflächen zur umgebenden Natur. Außen bilden sich durch Umrisslinien und Neigung des Daches Nischen unterschiedlicher Größe. Der Baukörper besteht aus Holz und leistet den starken Winden optimal Widerstand. So erneuert sich die Tradition und erhält dank des minimalistischen Designs – das Mobiliar eingeschlossen – einen Hauch von Eleganz.*

Cabin Vardehaugen, Norway

2008

### Nature's refuge: a contemporary chalet
*Die zeitgenössische Hütte für den Rückzug in die Natur*

**Design:** Hangar Design Group

Joshua Tree is a mountain haven, a modern reinterpretation of the traditional ski chalet that is designed to be placed among the rocks and verdant plateaus of the Alps. The module combines natural wood with steel cladding and the skylights in the sloping roof allow occupants to admire snow-capped peaks or gaze at the Alpine sky. The warm and welcoming interior features white oak on the ceiling, walls and furniture to create a study in cleanliness and functionality that can be customised to the very last detail. Perfect for a young family or small groups of friends, Joshua Tree can fit a master bedroom, a guest bedroom, two bathrooms with shared shower and a living area with kitchen into just 34 sq m (370 sq ft).

*Das Modell Joshua Tree ist eine Unterkunft für große Höhenlagen und eine moderne Interpretation der typischen Berghütte. Es lässt sich ebenso auf den Grünflächen alpiner Hochebenen als auch auf Felsboden aufstellen. Die Naturholzfassade steht im Kontrast zu den stahlverkleideten Seitenwänden. Die großen Dachfenster rahmen beschneite Gipfel oder Himmelsausschnitte. Innen sind die Decke, die Wände und die Möbel mit Weißeichenholz verkleidet – ein Design, das eine warme, einladende Atmosphäre schafft. Der Innenraum steht ganz im Zeichen formaler Klarheit und Funktionalität: Auf nur 34 m² finden ein Raum mit einem Doppelbett, ein Zweibettzimmer, zwei Bäder mit einer gemeinsamen Dusche und eine Wohnküche Platz, das Haus eignet sich also für junge Familien oder Kleingruppen. Die Einrichtung ist maßgefertigt und bis ins kleinste Detail durchdacht.*

## A house that opens on itself
*Ein Haus, das sich öffnet, um den Raum zu bewohnen*

**Design:** Michael Jantzen

R-House was designed as an ecologically friendly vacation home. The material used in the construction of the house is accoya, a sustainable wood processed without toxic chemicals. The photovoltaic cells and wind turbine on the roof ensure energy autonomy, and the water supply is guaranteed by the collection of rainwater that can then be heated using the energy from the sun, propane gas or hydrogen. The living space features a circular design with bridges and moving walkways and is defined by four large screens that can be moved and reconfigured to enclose the core. Moving the exterior rotating panels can change the configuration of the house and, depending upon conditions, determine whether or not you open or close the house to the elements.

*Das R-House wurde als umweltfreundliches und sich selbst mit Energie versorgendes Ferienhaus konzipiert. Als Baumaterial ist Accoya vorgesehen, eine Holzart, die nachhaltig und unter Verzicht auf giftige Pflanzenschutzmittel produziert wird. Fotovoltaikzellen und eine Windturbine auf dem Dach sollen für gefüllte Energiespeicher sorgen. Für die Wasserversorgung ist ein System zur Sammlung von Regenwasser geplant, wobei die Wassererwärmung mittels Solarenergie, Propangas oder Wasserstoff erfolgen soll. Der kreisförmige Wohnraum mit beweglichen Brücken und Laufstegen wird von vier großen, zu öffnenden Wänden definiert: Um die Form des Hauses zu verändern, braucht man lediglich die Wände zu verstellen und sich – je nach klimatischen Bedingungen – für einen geschlossenen oder offenen Raum zu entscheiden.*

## R-House, USA 2008

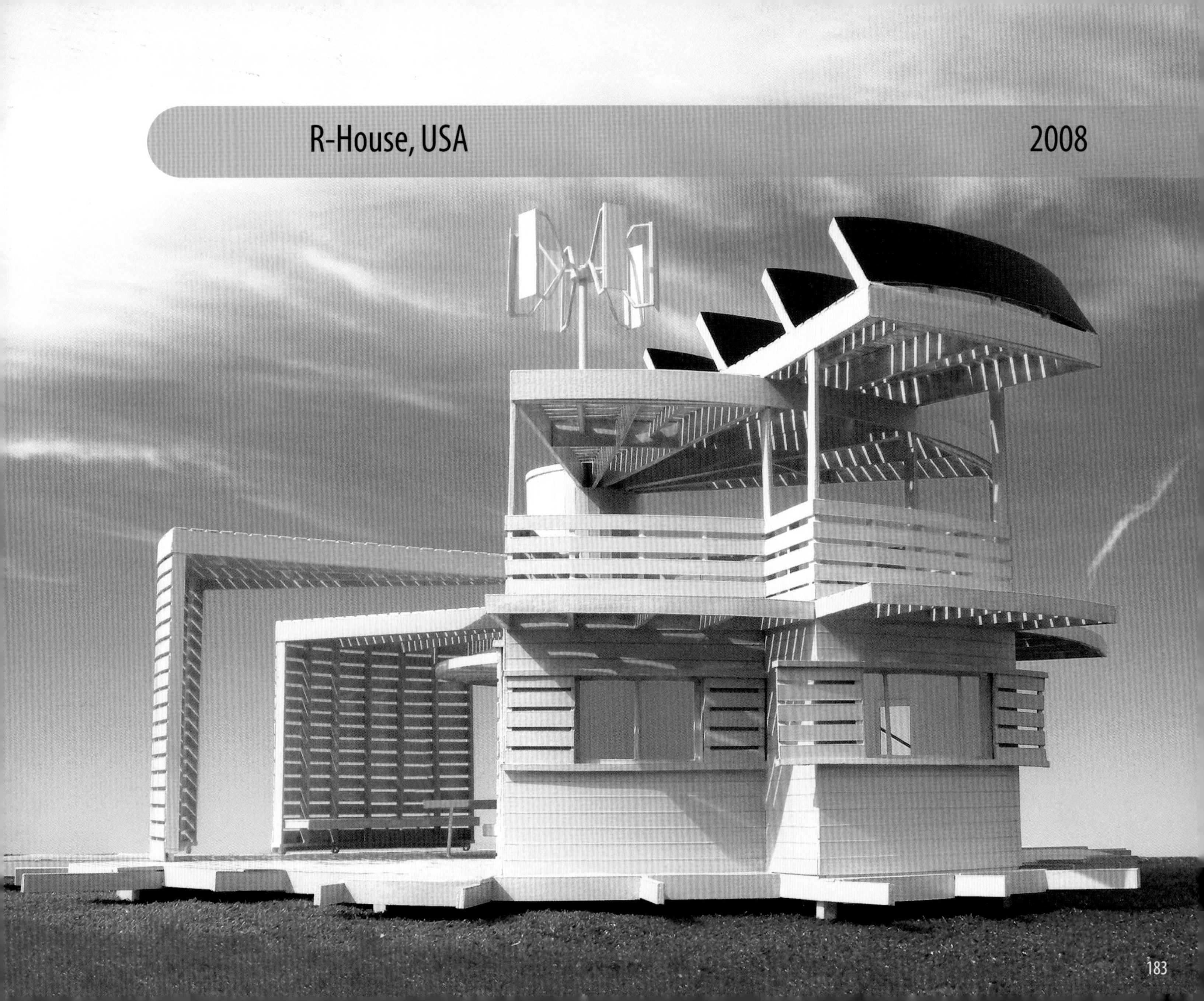

**Urban materials take on natural form**
*Städtische Materialien werden zu Formen der Natur*

**Design:** Recetas Urbanas

What at first glance looks like a giant mechanical spider is actually a mobile home unit. Created from standard materials used in an unusual way, Araña is a prime example of how creative recycling can give new life to items that were apparently of no further use. The futuristic arachnid-like structure is installed in urban environments, lifted off the ground by large crane arms for legs. With a similar feel to a tree house, it gives the impression of being suspended over the city. The basic module is a shipping container, which makes up the nucleus of the living space, but it can also connect to other small structures that serve as a kitchen or bathroom. Araña can be used as a dwelling or an office. To move it, the steel frame of "legs" is simply dismantled and the container is placed on a truck.

*Was auf den ersten Blick wie eine gewaltige mechanische Spinne aussieht, ist tatsächlich ein mobiles Haus aus ungewöhnlich eingesetzten Standard-Baumaterialien. Es beweist, dass kreatives, originelles Recycling auch scheinbar wertlosen Dingen zu einem zweiten Leben verhelfen kann. Araña wirkt im urbanen Kontext wie eine futuristische Vision: Starke Arme heben es gleich einem Kran in die Höhe, sodass man meint, darin über der Stadt zu schweben. Das Grundmodul besteht aus einem bewohnbaren Container, an den sich kleinere, als Küche und Bad nutzbare Teile anschließen können. Araña dient als Wohnung oder Büro. Um es an einem anderen Ort aufzustellen, muss nur das tragende Stahlgerüst abgebaut und auf einen Lastwagen geladen werden: eine Art Baumhaus in der Stadt oder ein mobiles Penthouse.*

# 186

**Temporary hotel**
*Ein temporäres Hotel*

**Design:** Tim Pyne

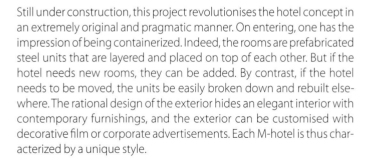

Still under construction, this project revolutionises the hotel concept in an extremely original and pragmatic manner. On entering, one has the impression of being containerized. Indeed, the rooms are prefabricated steel units that are layered and placed on top of each other. But if the hotel needs new rooms, they can be added. By contrast, if the hotel needs to be moved, the units be easily broken down and rebuilt elsewhere. The rational design of the exterior hides an elegant interior with contemporary furnishings, and the exterior can be customised with decorative film or corporate advertisements. Each M-hotel is thus characterized by a unique style.

*Dieses originelle und ausgesprochen funktionale Architekturprojekt, das sich zurzeit noch in der Realisierungsphase befindet, revolutioniert die traditionelle Vorstellung eines Hotels. Beim Eintreten wird man sich wie in einem Container fühlen: Die Zimmer bestehen aus vorgefertigten, auf- und nebeneinanderplatzierten Stahlmodulen. Bei Bedarf können jederzeit weitere Räume angefügt werden. Um das Hotel an einem anderen Ort aufzustellen, kann man die Einheiten einfach wieder abbauen. Die rationalistische, auf das Wesentliche reduzierte Außengestaltung wirkt im Innenbereich dank eines zeitgenössischen Einrichtungsstils elegant. Die Außenwände können mit dekorativen Transparenten oder Werbeplakaten versehen werden: So erhält jedes M-Hotel seinen individuellen Stil.*

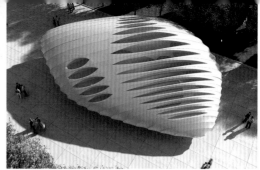

## The urban cloud embraces both past and present
*Eine Wolke in der Stadt spricht von Vergangenheit und Zukunft*

**Design:** Zaha Hadid

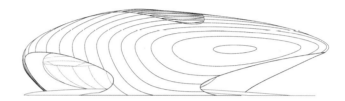

The Burnham Pavilion by renowned designer Zaha Hadid is a multimedia installation designed to mark the centennial of Daniel Burnham's 1909 urban plan for Chicago – a plan that forever changed the face of the city. The futuristic structure, whose shape resembles a cloud or a shell, is constructed of curved aluminum and covered by tensioned fabric. The pleated exterior is backlit at night (in changing colors) and the interior is used to screen centennial-themed videos that show the modern history of the city. The designer also sought to mitigate the environmental impact of the project: The pavilion can be dismantled, moved and reused and is made from recyclable materials.

*Burnham Pavilion entstand als multimediale Installation anlässlich des 100-jährigen Bestehens des Bebauungsplans von Daniel Burnham, der Chicago ein neues Gesicht verlieh. Ebenso zukunftsträchtig stellt sich dieser Bau dar, der nachts dank eines ausgeklügelten Lichtspiels die Farbe wechselt. Seine Form erinnert an eine Wolke oder eine Muschel. Die raffiniert gebogene Konstruktion aus Stahl und Aluminium ruft eine beeindruckende dynamische Wirkung hervor, während die Verkleidung mit einem technischen Spezialgewebe die Faltenstruktur zusätzlich betont. Im Innenraum werden Videos und Filme zur Entwicklungsgeschichte der Stadt gezeigt. Die bekannte Architektin Zaha Hadid hat sich um weitestgehende Umweltverträglichkeit bemüht: Der Pavillon kann abgebaut und an anderer Stelle neu genutzt werden, außerdem sind alle eingesetzten Materialien wiederverwendbar.*

# photo credits

**Airstream Trailers** (www.airstream.com) – pp. 4 (first from left), 15, 28, 29: courtesy of Airstream, Inc.

**Aktion Poliphile** (www.studiogranda.is) – pp. 5 (fifth from left), 84, 85: Norbert Miguletz, Studio Granda

**Araña** (www.recetasurbanas.net) – pp. 184, 185: courtesy of Recetas Urbanas

**Bookbus** (www.muungano.com) – pp. 156, 157, 158, 159: courtesy of Clive Tompsett, Muungano

**Cabin Vardehaugen** (www.fantasticnorway.com) – pp. 12-13, 176, 177, 178, 179: courtesy of Arne Michal Paulsen, Fantastic Norway

**Camion Inox** (www.jeannouvel.fr) – p.86: courtesy of Ateliers Jean Nouvel; pp. 87, 88, 89: © Philippe Ruault

**Capa Self Sustained Module** (www.cannatafernandes.com) – pp. 130, 131, 132, 133: courtesy of Luís Ferreira Alves, Cannatà & Fernandes

**Caravan Laverda "Serie blu"** (www.epidesign.it) – pp. 5 (sixth from left), 62, 63: courtesy of Enrico Picciani, Nizzoli Sistemi

**Casa Insecto** (www.recetasurbanas.net) – pp. 5 (second from left), 118, 119: courtesy of Santiago Cirugeda

**Casa Minolina 51** (www.arc.usi.ch) – pp. 42, 43: Fondo Giulio Minoletti, Archivio del Moderno, Mendrisio

**DST Self Sustained Module** (www.cannatafernandes.com) – pp. 6 (fifth from left), 134, 135, 136, 137: courtesy of Luís Ferreira Alves, Cannatà & Fernandes

**Farnsworth House** (www.farnsworthhouse.org) – p. 30 top © Alan Weintraub/Arcaid/Corbis; p. 30 bottom © Alan Weintraub/Arcaid/Corbis; p. 31 © Alan Weintraub/Arcaid/Corbis. Thanks to Farnsworth House. A National Trust Historic Site

**Flake House** (www.olgga.fr) – pp. 6 (fourth from left), 160 bottom, 161: courtesy of olgga architectes; p. 160 top: Fabienne Delafraye

**FRED** (www.olkruf.com) – pp. 110, 111: Ignacio Martinez, Arch. di. Oskar Leo Kaufmann – Albert Rüf Ziviltechniker GmbH

**FREITAG Shop Zürich** (www.freitag.ch) – pp. 7 (fifth from left), 11, 152, 153: courtesy of Roland Tännler, Spillmann Echsle, FREITAG

**Future Shack** (www.seangodsell.com) – pp. 78, 79: courtesy of Sean Godsell Architects

**Geodesic Dome** (www.buckminsterfuller.com) – pp. 40 (bottom left), 50, 51: courtesy of The Estate of R. Buckminster Fuller

**Glass House between Sea and Sky** (www.jade.dti.ne.jp/shoeiyoh) – pp. 90, 91: courtesy of Shoei Yoh Hamura

**Glidehouse®** (www.mkd-arc.com) – pp. 138, 139, 140, 141: courtesy of John Swain Photography, Michelle Kaufmann

**Hollywood Houses** (www.schulitz.de) – pp. 76, 77: courtesy of Helmut C. Schulitz

**House in Beverly Hills** (www.schulitz.de) – pp. 64, 65, 66, 67: courtesy of Helmut C. Schulitz

**House of Steel and Wood** (www.ecosistemaurbano.com) – pp. 142, 143: courtesy of Emilio P. Doiztua, Ecosistema urbano

**Joshua Tree** (www.hangardesigngroup.com) – pp. 8 top, 116 top left, 180, 181: courtesy of Hangar Design Group

**Kaufmann Desert House** (www.kaufmanndeserthouse.com) – pp. 5 (fourth from left), 16 bottom, 33: © Walter Bibikow/JAI/Corbis; p. 32 top © Alan Weintraub/Arcaid/Corbis; p. 32 bottom © Alan Weintraub/Arcaid/Corbis

**LoftCube** (www.loftcube.net) – pp. 115, 144, 145: courtesy of Steffen Jaenicke, LoftCube GmbH

**Lustron Homes** (www.lustronconnection.org) – pp. 34, 35, 36, 37: courtesy of Peter A. Rogers

**MagicKub, "b(R)ouillon architectural"** (www.atelierrvl.com) – pp. 162, 163, 164, 165: courtesy of Clément Darrasse, Jean-Charles Liddell. Thanks to Philippe Tardits, Pierre Alexadre Cochez (landscape architect), Marcel Roulet (wood ingenior) and Michel Robin (aluminium doors and windows, iron-mongery)

**Maison à Coutras** (www.lacatonvassal.com) – pp. 72 bottom, 104, 105: courtesy of © Philippe Ruault

**Maison à Lège, Cap Ferret** (www.lacatonvassal.com) – p. 96: bottom courtesy of Lacaton & Vassal; pp. 96 top, 97: courtesy of © Philippe Ruault

**Maison flottante** (www.bouroullec.com) – pp. 7 (second from left), 120, 121, 123: courtesy of © Paul Tahon and R & E Bouroullec; p. 122: courtesy of © www.gaelleleboulicaut.com

**Markies** (www.bohtlingk.nl) – pp. 6 (sixth from left), 72 top, 80, 81, 82, 83: courtesy of Roos Aldershoff (Amsterdam), Eduard Böhtlingk

**MDU (Mobile Dwelling Unit)** (www.lot-ek.com) – pp. 6 (third from left), 124, 125: courtesy of the Walker Art Center, LOT-EK

**Mercury House One** (www.architectureandvision.com) – pp. 10, 168, 169: courtesy of © Architecture and Vision

**M&G Ricerche** (www.samynandpartners.be) – pp. 6 (first from left), 72 middle, 92, 93, 94, 95: courtesy of © PROJECT: Philippe Samyn and Partners / PHOTO: Matteo Piazza

**M-Hotel** (www.timpyne.com) – pp. 186, 187: courtesy of Tim Pyne

**M-House** (www.michaeljantzen.com) – pp. 112, 113: Michael Jantzen

**M-House** (www.timpyne.com) – pp. 116 (bottom left), 126, 127, 128, 129: courtesy of Tim Pyne

**Millennium Dome** (www.rsh-p.com) – pp. 100, 101: © Grant Smith

**Mini House** (www.minihouse.se) – pp. 6 (second from left), 170, 171: courtesy of Andy Liffner, Jonas Wagell

**Mobile House** (www.ihd.it) – pp. 58, 59: courtesy of Isao Hosoe; pp. 60, 61: courtesy of Valerio Castelli

**Modular House Mobile** (www.ateliervanlieshout.com) – pp. 98, 99: Atelier Van Lieshout

**Mukarov House** (www.ivankroupa.cz) – pp. 106, 107: courtesy of Arne Valen, Ivan Kroupa

**Nakagin Capsule Tower** (www.kisho.co.jp) – pp. 40 (top left), 52, 53, 54, 55: courtesy of Kisho Kurokawa architect & associates, Tomio Ohashi

**OMD ShowHouse** (www.designmobile.com) – pp. 8 middle, 148, 149, 150, 151: courtesy of OMD, Jennifer Siegal

**PUMA City** (www.lot-ek.com) – pp. 7 (sixth from left), 172, 173, 174, 175: courtesy of Danny Bright, LOT-EK

**R-House** (www.michaeljantzen.com) – pp. 7 (third from left), 182, 183: Michael Jantzen

**Santa Monica Prefab** (www.designmobile.com) – pp. 8 bottom, 166, 167: courtesy of OMD, Jennifer Siegal

**Six-Shell-Bubble** (www.knitz.net) – pp. 7 (fourth from left), 39, 49: courtesy of Andreas Knitz; p. 48 top: courtesy of Wiebke Elzel and Rebecca Wilton; p. 48 bottom: courtesy of Lüdenscheid city archive (Werner Siller), Andreas Knitz

**Stainless House with Light Lattice** (www.jade.dti.ne.jp/shoeiyoh) – pp. 74, 75: courtesy of Shoei Yoh Hamura

**Superadobe Domes and Vaults** (www.calearth.org) – pp. 4 (sixth from left), 116 top right, 146, 147: courtesy of Cal-Earth Institute

**SU-SI** (www.olkruf.com) – pp. 102, 103: Ignacio Martinez, Arch. di. Oskar Leo Kaufmann – Albert Rüf Ziviltechniker GmbH

**Teatro del mondo** (www.fondazionealdorossi.org) – pp. 4 (fourth from left), 40 (top right), 68, 69: © Eredi Aldo Rossi

**The Burnham Pavilion** (www.zaha-hadid.com) – pp. 188 top left, 189: courtesy of TheGrayCircle.com; p. 188 top right and bottom: courtesy of Zaha Hadid Architects

**The Good, the Bad and the Ugly** (www.ateliervanlieshout.com) – pp. 71, 108, 109: Atelier Van Lieshout

**Tipi Tents** – pp. 4 (fifth from left), 19: Istockphoto (Yails); p. 18 left: Istockphoto (Jeanell Norvell); p. 18 right: Istockphoto (xyno)

**Unità di emergenza Fiat-Anic** (www.arc.usi.ch) – pp. 56, 57: Fondo Marco Zanuso, Archivio del Moderno, Mendrisio

**Volkner Mobil Performance** (www.volkner-mobil.com) – pp. 7 (first from left), 154, 155: courtesy of Volkner Mobil GmbH

**Volkswagen-Transporter** (www.volkswagen.com) – pp. 5 (first from left), 44, 45, 46, 47: courtesy of Volkswagen Group

**Wagon Trains** – pp. 4 (second from left), 16 (middle), 25: Istockphoto (ericfoltz); p. 24 left: Istockphoto (ftwitty); p. 24 right: Istockphoto (Primeop76)

**Yurts** – pp. 5 (third from left), 16 top, 20, 21, 22-23: courtesy of Raffaele Brustia

**4 D Dymaxion House** (www.buckminsterfuller.com) – pp. 4 (third from left), 26, 27: courtesy of The Estate of R. Buckminster Fuller

**Cover pictures**. Front cover: Volkswagen-Transporter (courtesy of Volkswagen Group); Backcover, from left: Mercury House One (courtesy of ©Architecture and Vision), Six-Shell-Bubble (courtesy of Andreas Knitz).

**Donato Nappo** was born in Salerno in 1970. He holds a degree in architecture from the Polytechnic of Milan and specialized in Industrial Design at the University of Florence. For years he has worked as a professional designer in the automotive sector.

**Stefania Vairelli** was born in Alexandria in 1975. She has worked for years in the world of design and communications where her studies have found literary and artistic expression.

Both are students of life and contemporary lifestyles, fascinated in particular by the concept of mobility and the nomadic way of life. They live and work in Italy.

***Donato Nappo,** 1970 in Salerno geboren, hat am Polytechnikum Mailand Architektur studiert und sich anschließend an der Universität Florenz auf Industriedesign spezialisiert. Seit vielen Jahren ist er als Designer in der Automobilbranche tätig.*

***Stefania Vairelli** wurde 1975 in Alessandria geboren. Literatur- und Kunststudien lenkten ihren beruflichen Weg in die Welt des Designs und der Kommunikation, in der sie seit Jahren zu Hause ist.*

*Ihr Interesse gilt dem zeitgenössischen Leben und Wohnen, und hier vor allem den Konzepten der Mobilität und des Nomadentums. Beide leben und arbeiten in Italien.*